The British Novel:
Scott Through Hardy

GOLDENTREE BIBLIOGRAPHIES
IN LANGUAGE AND LITERATURE

under the series editorship of

O. B. HARDISON, JR.

AFRO-AMERICAN WRITERS • Darwin T. Turner

AGE OF DRYDEN, THE • Donald F. Bond

AMERICAN DRAMA FROM ITS BEGINNINGS TO THE PRESENT •
E. Hudson Long

AMERICAN LITERATURE: POE THROUGH GARLAND • Harry Hayden Clark

AMERICAN LITERATURE THROUGH BRYANT • Richard Beale Davis

AMERICAN NOVEL, THE: SINCLAIR LEWIS TO THE PRESENT • Blake Nevius

AMERICAN NOVEL THROUGH HENRY JAMES, THE • C. Hugh Holman

BRITISH NOVEL, THE: CONRAD TO THE PRESENT • Paul J. Wiley

BRITISH NOVEL, THE: SCOTT THROUGH HARDY • Ian Watt

CHAUCER • Albert C. Baugh

LINGUISTICS AND ENGLISH LINGUISTICS • Harold B. Allen

LITERARY CRITICISM: PLATO THROUGH JOHNSON • Vernon Hall

MILTON • James Holly Hanford

OLD AND MIDDLE ENGLISH LITERATURE • William Matthews

ROMANTIC POETS AND PROSE WRITERS • Richard Harter Fogle

SIXTEENTH CENTURY, THE: SKELTON THROUGH HOOKER • John L. Lievsay

TUDOR AND STUART DRAMA • Irving Ribner

VICTORIAN POETS AND PROSE WRITERS • Jerome H. Buckley

FORTHCOMING TITLES

BRITISH NOVEL THROUGH JANE AUSTEN, THE • Wayne C. Booth &
Gwin J. Kolb

EIGHTEENTH CENTURY, THE • Donald F. Bond

SEVENTEENTH CENTURY, THE: BACON THROUGH MARVELL •
Arthur E. Barker

SHAKESPEARE

The British Novel: Scott Through Hardy

compiled by

Ian Watt

Stanford University

AHM PUBLISHING CORPORATION
Northbrook, Illinois 60062

ISBN: 0-88295-533-0

Library of Congress Card Number: 72-96559

PRINTED IN THE UNITED STATES OF AMERICA

733-1

Preface

THE FOLLOWING BIBLIOGRAPHY is intended for graduate and advanced undergraduate students who desire a convenient guide to scholarship in the field of Victorian fiction. The listing is necessarily selective, but every effort has been made to provide ample coverage of major authors and topics, with emphasis on work published in the twentieth century. The novelists included are those whose main output comes after 1817 (the death of Jane Austen—thus Maria Edgeworth and Maturin are excluded) but before 1890 (thus George Gissing and George Moore are in the *Conrad to the Present* bibliography).

In order to keep the bibliography to a reasonable size, the following have been omitted: unpublished dissertations; general literary histories and bibliographies; short notes and explications (except when they contain exceptionally important data); and older studies now largely superseded by later work. The cross-references do not include such obvious sources as histories of the novel, or, under a particular novel, a general study of its author already listed above. Paperback editions of novels are only recorded as such if they seem of exceptional merit, if they make available novels one might not expect to be in print, or if the introductions are of unusual interest.

In a few matters I have departed from the usual format of the series so as to take account of the special nature of Victorian fiction. In order to draw attention to many novelists of some stature who are now little known, I have treated some eighty of them in the alphabetical listing of individual novelists. As a reminder of the voluminous output of many of them, and of the way they were often published, I have listed the full-length novels of some of the major novelists, and given details if they were published in serial or number form. For other novelists I have given only a short list of novels, usually without details of

v

publication. Even so, the number of Victorian novelists is so great that the bibliography is supplemented by a concluding section of some hundred other novelists listed by name and dates only; this list, incidentally, includes writers of fiction, such as Cardinal Newman, whose main achievements—and bibliography—are to be found elsewhere. Short stories and children's fiction, both very characteristic of the period, have not been covered.

In general, the bibliography steers a middle course between the brief lists of references included in the average textbook and the long professional bibliography in which the most significant items are often lost in the sheer number of references given.

Attention is called to three useful features:
(1) The wide margin on each page permits listing of library call numbers.
(2) The space at the bottom of every other page permits inclusion of additional entries, and there are blank pages for notes at the end.
(3) The index and cross-reference numbers conveniently key the reader to the appropriate entry in the text.

Other annotations are: in square brackets—additions to the facts of publication; in parentheses—editorial description or comment on a title. An asterisk following an entry indicates a work of unusual importance or interest. A dagger (†) indicates a paperback edition.

Symbols identifying journals follow, insofar as possible, the forms given in the Table of Symbols at the beginning of the annual *PMLA* bibliography. The symbols and their meanings are as follows:

AI	American Imago
AL	American Literature
AR	Antioch Review
BB	Bulletin of Bibliography
BJRL	Bulletin of the John Rylands Library
BST	Brontë Society Transactions
BSTCF	Ball State Teachers College Forum
BUSE	Boston University Studies in Literature
CE	College English
CentR	Centennial Review

CL	Comparative Literature
CLS	Comparative Literature Studies
ContempR	Contemporary Review
CQR	Church Quarterly Review
CR	Critical Review
CritQ	Critical Quarterly
CSE	Cornell Studies in English
DiS	Dickens Studies
DR	Dalhousie Review
EA	Etudes Anglaises
E&S	Essays and Studies by Members of the English Association
EDH	Essays by Divers Hands
EdinUJ	Edinburgh University Journal
EFT	English Fiction in Transition
EIC	Essays in Criticism
EJ	English Journal
EL	Everyman's Library
ELH	Journal of English Literary History
ELN	English Langue Notes
ELT	English Literature in Transition (1880–1920)
ES	English Studies
ESA	English Studies in Africa
ForumH	Forum (Houston)
FR	French Review
HLQ	Huntington Library Quarterly
HudR	Hudson Review
JEcon	Journal of Economics
JEGP	Journal of English and Germanic Philology
JPC	Journal of Popular Culture
KR	Kenyon Review
LitM	Literary Monographs (Madison, Wisconsin)
LMerc	London Mercury
LQHR	London Quarterly and Holborn Review
MFS	Modern Fiction Studies
MLN	Modern Language Notes
MLQ	Modern Language Quarterly
MLR	Modern Language Review
MP	Modern Philology
MR	Massachusetts Review
N&Q	Notes and Queries
NCF	Nineteenth-Century Fiction
NDQ	North Dakota Quarterly
NM	Neuphilologische Mitteilungen
NS	Die Neueren Sprachen
OUR	Ohio University Review
PBSA	Papers of the Bibliographical Society of America
PLL	Papers on Language and Literature
PMLA	Publications of the Modern Language Association
PP	Philologica Pragensia

PQ	Philological Quarterly
PR	Partisan Review
PsyR	Psychoanalytic Review
PULC	Princeton University Library Chronicle
QQ	Queen's Quarterly
QR	Quarterly Review
RDM	Revue des Deux Mondes
REL	Review of English Literature
RES	Review of English Studies
RLC	Revue de Littérature Comparée
RLitC	Readings in Literary Criticism Series
RLV	Revue des Langues Vivantes
RMS	Renaissance & Modern Studies
SAQ	South Atlantic Quarterly
SB	Studies in Bibliography: Papers of the Bibliographical Society of the University of Virginia
SEL	Studies in English Literature, 1500–1900
SEngL	Studies in English Literature
SoR	Southern Review
SP	Studies in Philology
SR	Sewanee Review
SSF	Studies in Short Fiction
SSL	Studies in Scottish Literature
TCI	Twentieth Century Interpretations
TCV	Twentieth Century Views
TEAS	Twayne's English Author Series
TLS	Times Literary Supplement
TQ	Texas Quarterly
TSLL	Texas Studies in Literature and Language
UCPES	U. of Calif. Pubs., English Studies
UKCR	University of Kansas City Review
UKPHS	U. of Kansas Pubs., Humanistic Studies
UNCSCL	U. of N. C. Studies in Comparative Literature
UTQ	University of Toronto Quarterly
UTSE	University of Texas Studies in English
VN	Victorian Newsletter
VQR	Virginia Quarterly Review
VS	Victorian Studies
WC	World's Classics
WHR	Western Humanities Review
WTW	Writers and Their Work
WVUPP	West Virginia University Philological Papers
YR	Yale Review
YSE	Yale Studies in English
YULG	Yale University Library Gazette

ch.	chapter
comp.,comps.	compiler, compilers
ed.	edited by, edition

enl.	enlarged
fl.	*floruit,* flourished
mag.	magazine
n.s.	new series
P	Press
pseud.	pseudonym
pub.	published, publisher
repr.	reprint, reprinted
rev.	revised
trans.	translated
U	University
U P	University Press
vol., vols.	volume, volumes

I am much indebted to those who have helped me in preparing this bibliography—Peter Hoff, Roger and Carol Henkle, Anne Friedlander, Joy Weston, Mark Savin, and Jane Palmer; and also to John Raleigh, Ulrich Knoepflmacher, Robert Polhemus, David Fong, George Levine, Philip Collins, Masao Miyoshi, and the late Bradford Booth, who heroically detected and selflessly amended many of my innumerable errors of information or judgment.

NOTE: The publisher and compiler invite suggestions for additions to future editions of the bibliography.

Contents

Bibliographies, Journals, and Surveys of Scholarship

1 ALTICK, Richard D., and William R. MATTHEWS, comps. *Guide to Doctoral Dissertations in Victorian Literature, 1886-1958.* Urbana: U of Illinois P, 1960.

2 BATHO, Edith C., and Bonamy DOBRÉE. *The Victorians and After, 1830-1914.* [1938]. 3d. ed., London: Cresset, 1962. (General essays followed by selective bibliographies, with commentary.)

3 BELL, Inglis F., and Donald BAIRD. *The English Novel, 1578-1956: A Checklist of Twentieth-Century Criticisms.* Denver: Swallow, 1959.†

4 BLOCK, Andrew. *The English Novel, 1740-1850: A Catalogue* [1910]. Rev. ed., London: Dawsons, 1961. (Undependable.)

5 BUCKLEY, Jerome H. *Victorian Poets and Prose Writers.* Goldentree Bibliography. Northbrook, Ill.: AHM, 1966.

6 *Cambridge Bibliography of English Literature.* Ed. F. W. Bateson. Vol. III. Cambridge: Cambridge U P, 1941. Revised edition, ed. George Watson, 1800-1900, 1969.*

7 *Concise Cambridge Bibliography of English Literature, 600-1950* [1958]. Ed. George Watson. 2d ed., Cambridge: Cambridge U P, 1965.*

8 EHRSAM, Theodore G., and Robert H. DEILY, comps., under the direction of Robert M. Smith. *Bibliographies of Twelve Victorian Authors.* New York: Octagon, 1968. (Repr. of 1936 ed. Includes Hardy, Stevenson, and Swinburne.)

9 English Association. *The Year's Work in English Studies,* 1919- . London: Oxford U P. (Review of scholarly work of the previous year, including a chapter on the nineteenth century.)

10 "English IX. Nineteenth Century." In "MLA International Bibliography," *Publications of the Modern Language Association of America.* 1922- . (Standard listing of previous year's publications, including *Dissertation Abstracts.)**

11 *English Literature in Transition. 1880-1920.* [*English Fiction in Transition,* 1957-1962] 1962- . (Periodical; especially valuable for its annotated bibliographies of later writers.)

12 FOGLE, Richard Harter. *Romantic Poets and Prose Writers.* Goldentree Bibliography. Northbrook, Ill.: AHM, 1966.

13 HOUGHTON, Walter E., ed. *The Wellesley Index to Victorian Periodicals, 1824-1900.* Vol. 1. Toronto: U of Toronto P, 1966. (Identifies anonymous contributors to monthlies and quarterlies, including novel-reviewers.)

1

14 LECLAIRE, L. A. *General Analytical Bibliography of the Regional Novelists of the British Isles, 1800–1950*. Paris: Société d'Edition "Les Belles Lettres," 1954.

15 MC GARRY, Daniel D., and Sarah H. WHITE. *Historical Fiction Guide*. Metuchen, N. J.: Scarecrow, 1963.

16 *Modern Fiction Studies, 1955–* . ("Modern" often interpreted generously.)

17 Modern Humanities Research Association. *Annual Bibliography of English Language and Literature, 1920–* . Cambridge: Bowes & Bowes, 1920– .

18 *Nineteenth-Century Fiction, 1945–* . (Called *The Trollopian*, 1945–1949. Main periodical for Victorian fiction.)*

19 *Novel*, 1967– . (Periodical devoted entirely to longer fiction.)

20 RAY, Gordon N. *Bibliographical Resources for the Study of Nineteenth Century Fiction*. Los Angeles: School of Library Service, U of California, 1964.

21 "The Romantic Movement." (Annual listing of books and articles in *ELH* [1937–1949]; then in *PQ* [1950–1965]; and now in *ELN* Supplement [1966–].)

22 SADLEIR, Michael. *Excursions in Victorian Bibliography*. London: Chaundy & Cox, 1922. (Includes A. Trollope, Marryat, Disraeli, Collins, Reade, Whyte-Melville, Mrs. Gaskell.)

23 SADLEIR, Michael. *XIX Century Fiction: A Bibliographical Record Based on His Own Collection*. 2 vols. Berkeley: U of California P, 1951. (Also contains essays.)*

24 SLACK, Robert C., ed. *Bibliographies of Studies in Victorian Literature for the Ten Years 1955–1964*. Urbana: U of Illinois P, 1967. (Reproduces annual bibliographies published in *Modern Philology* [1956–1957] and *Victorian Studies* [1959–1965].) See 32.

25 STEVENSON, Lionel, ed. *Victorian Fiction: A Guide to Research*. Cambridge, Mass.: Harvard U P, 1964. (Surveys by specialists of scholarship on the main Victorian novelists.)*

26 *Studies in English Literature, 1961–* . (Autumn issue annually includes an article reviewing "Recent Studies in Nineteenth-Century Literature" by a specialist.)

27 TEMPLEMAN, William D., ed. *Bibliographies of Studies in Victorian Literature, 1932–1944*. Urbana: U of Illinois P, 1945. (Annual lists collected from *Modern Philology*; indexed.)

28 THURSTON, Jarvis, et al. *Short Fiction Criticism: A Checklist of Interpretation since 1925 of Stories and Novelettes (American, British, Continental) 1800–1958*. Denver: Swallow, 1960.

29 "Victorian Bibliography." Annual listing of books and articles in *Modern Philology* (1933–1957) and thereafter in *Victorian Studies* (1958–). See 24.*

30 *Victorian Newsletter, 1953–* . (Semiannual bibliography.)

31 WALKER, Warren S. *Twentieth-Century Short Story Explication; Interpretations, 1900–1960 Inclusive, of Short Fiction since 1800.* Hamden, Conn.: Shoe String P, 1961. (Suppls., 1963, 1965.)

32 WRIGHT, Austin. *Bibliographies of Studies in Victorian Literature, 1945–1954.* Urbana: U of Illinois P, 1956. (Annual lists collected from *Modern Philology;* indexed.) See 24.

Literary Histories

33 ALLEN, Walter. *The English Novel.* New York: Dutton, 1955.*†

34 BAKER, E. A. *The History of the English Novel.* 10 vols. London: Witherby, 1924–1939. Vol. 6, *Edgeworth, Austen, Scott;* Vol 7, *The Age of Dickens and Thackeray;* Vol. 8, *From the Brontës to Meredith: Romanticism in the English Novel;* Vol. 9, *The Day before Yesterday* (includes Hardy, "Mark Rutherford," etc.)*

35 DELAFIELD, E. M. [pseud.]. *Ladies and Gentlemen of Victorian Fiction.* London: Hogarth, 1937.

36 DE LA MARE, Walter, ed. *The Eighteen-Eighties.* Cambridge: Cambridge U P, 1930.

37 DRINKWATER, John, ed. *The Eighteen-Sixties.* Cambridge: Cambridge U P, 1932.

38 FLANAGAN, Thomas B. *The Irish Novelists 1800–1850.* New York: Columbia U P, 1959.

39 FORD, Boris, ed. *The Pelican Guide to English Literature.* Baltimore: Penguin, 1957. (Vol. V, *From Blake to Byron;* Vol. VI, *From Dickens to Hardy.*)†

40 FRIERSON, W. C. *The English Novel in Transition, 1885–1940.* Norman: U of Oklahoma P, 1942.

41 GRANVILLE-BARKER, H., ed. *The Eighteen-Seventies.* Cambridge: Cambridge U P, 1929.

42 KARL, Frederick R. *An Age of Fiction: The Nineteenth Century British Novel.* New York: Farrar, Straus, & Giroux, 1964.

43 MARSHALL, Percy. *Masters of the English Novel.* London: Dobson, 1962.

44 SAINTSBURY, George. *The English Novel.* New York: Dutton, 1913.

45 STEVENSON, Lionel. *The English Novel: A Panorama.* Boston: Houghton Mifflin, 1960.†

46 WAGENKNECHT, Edward. *Cavalcade of the English Novel* [1943]. Rev. ed., New York: Holt, 1954.*

General Critical Studies and Collections

47 ALLOTT, Miriam. *Novelists on the Novel*. New York: Columbia U P, 1959. (Extensive collection of writings arranged under critical headings, with introduction.)†

48 BARTLETT, Lynn C., and William R. SHERWOOD. *The English Novel: Background Readings*. Philadelphia and New York: Lippincott, 1967. (Collects contemporary reviews, letters, etc., about novels including *Heart of Midlothian, Wuthering Heights, Vanity Fair, Bleak House, Middlemarch, Jude the Obscure*.)†

49 BOOTH, Wayne C. *The Rhetoric of Fiction*. Chicago and London: U of Chicago P, 1961.*†

50 BROWN, E. K. *Rhythm in the Novel*. Toronto: U of Toronto P, 1950.†

51 BUCKLER, William E., ed. *Minor Classics of Nineteenth-Century Fiction*. 2 vols. Boston: Houghton Mifflin, 1967. (Reprints many novels and short stories, including some not otherwise available in paperback, such as Elizabeth Gaskell's *Cranford*, James Hogg's *The Private Memoirs and Confessions of a Justified Sinner*, William Hale White's *The Autobiography of Mark Rutherford*.)†

52 CECIL, Lord David. *Victorian Novelists: Essays in Revaluation*. Chicago: U of Chicago P, 1958. [First pub. as *Early Victorian Novelists*, 1935.]†

53 COLBY, Robert A. *Fiction with a Purpose: Major and Minor Nineteenth Century Novels*, Bloomington: Indiana U P, 1967.

54 COOK, Albert. *The Meaning of Fiction*. Detroit: Wayne State U P, 1960.

55 CROFT-COOKE, Rupert. *Feasting with Panthers: A New Consideration of Some Late Victorian Writers*. London: Allen & Unwin, 1967.

56 DAVIS, Robert G. "The Sense of the Real in English Fiction." *CL*, 3(1951):200-17.

57 DE LA MARE, Walter. "Some Women Novelists," *Pleasures and Speculations*. London: Faber, 1940.

58 DONOVAN, Robert Alan. *The Shaping Vision: Imagination in the English Novel from Defoe to Dickens*. Ithaca: Cornell U P, 1966.

59 DREW, Elizabeth. *The Novel: A Modern Guide to Fifteen English Masterpieces*. New York: Norton, 1964.†

60 EAKER, Jay Gordon. "Emergent Modernism in Late Victorian Fiction." *SAQ*, 44(1945):286-93.

61 ELWIN, Malcolm. *Old Gods Falling*. New York: Macmillan, 1939.

62 ELWIN, Malcolm. *Victorian Wallflowers*. London: Cape, 1934. (Concerns minor writers.)

63   FORSTER, E. M. *Aspects of the Novel.* New York: Harcourt, Brace, 1927.†

64   FRIEDMAN, Alan. *The Turn of the Novel.* New York: Oxford U P, 1966. (The "turn" begins with Hardy.)

65   FRIEDMAN, Norman. "The Point of View in Fiction: The Development of a Critical Concept." *PMLA*, 70(1955):1160-84.

66   GRAHAM, Kenneth. *English Criticism of the Novel, 1865-1900.* New York: Oxford U P; Oxford: Clarendon P, 1965.

67   HARDY, Barbara. *The Appropriate Form: An Essay on the Novel.* London: Athlone, 1964. (On James, Defoe, C. Brontë, Hardy, Forster, Meredith, Eliot, D. H. Lawrence, Tolstoy.)*

68   HARRISON, Frederic. *Studies in Early Victorian Literature.* London: Arnold, 1895. (Includes essays on C. Brontë, Dickens, Disraeli, George Eliot, and Thackeray.)

69   HARVEY, W. J. *Character and the Novel.* Ithaca: Cornell U P, 1965.*

70   KERMODE, Frank. *The Sense of an Ending: Studies in the Theory of Fiction.* New York: Oxford U P, 1967.†

71   KETTLE, Arnold. *An Introduction to the English Novel.* 2 vols. London and New York: Hutchinson, 1951-1953.*†

72   LEAVIS, F. R. *The Great Tradition.* London: Chatto & Windus, 1948. (George Eliot, Dickens.)*†

73   LEVINE, George L. *The Boundaries of Fiction: Carlyle, Macaulay, Newman.* Princeton: Princeton U P, 1968.

74   LODGE, David. *Language of Fiction: Essays in Criticism and Verbal Analysis of the English Novel.* New York: Columbia U P, 1966.

75   LUBBOCK, Percy. *The Craft of Fiction.* New York: Scribner's, 1921.*†

76   LUKÁCS, Georg. *Realism in Our Time: Literature and the Class Struggle.* Trans. John and Necke Mauder. New York: Harper & Row, 1964. (By the greatest of modern Marxist critics.)*

77   MARSHALL, William H. *The World of the Victorian Novel.* Cranbury, N.J.: Barnes, 1967.

78   MARTIN, Harold C., ed. *Style in Prose Fiction.* English Institute Essays. New York: Columbia U P, 1959.

79   MASSINGHAM, H. J. and Hugh, eds. *The Great Victorians.* 2 vols. London: Nicholson & Watson, 1932.

80   MELVILLE, Lewis [pseud.]. *Victorian Novelists.* London: Constable, 1906.

81   MENDILOW, A. A. *Time and the Novel.* London and New York: Nevill, 1952.

82   MILLER, J. Hillis. "Some Implications of Form in Victorian Fiction," *CLS*, 3(1966):109-18.

83   MUIR, Edwin. *The Structure of the Novel.* London: Hogarth, 1928.

84   MYERS, Walter L. *The Later Realism. A Study of Characterization in the British Novel.* Chicago: U of Chicago P, 1927.

85 OLIPHANT, James A. *Victorian Novelists*. London: Blackie, 1899.

86 OLIPHANT, Margaret, ed. *Women Novelists of Queen Victoria's Reign.* London: Hurst & Blackett, 1877. (Appreciations by Mrs. Oliphant, Mrs. Lynn Linton, Mrs. Alexander, et al.)

87 PRITCHETT, V. S. *The Living Novel and Later Appreciations.* New York: Random House, 1964. (Incorporates essays from *The Living Novel* [1947] and *The Working Novelist* [1965].)*†

88 RATHBURN, Robert C., and Martin STEINMANN, Jr., eds. *From Jane Austen to Joseph Conrad.* Minneapolis: U of Minnesota P, 1958.†

89 REID, Forrest. "Minor Fiction in the 'Eighties.' " *The Eighteen-Eighties.* Ed. Walter de la Mare. Cambridge: Cambridge U P, 1930.

90 ROMBERG, Bertil. *Studies in the Narrative Technique of the First-Person Novel.* Stockholm: Almquist & Wiksell, 1962. (Occasional references to Scott, Dickens, Thackeray, the Brontës.)

91 SCHORER, Mark, ed. *Society and Self in the Novel.* English Institute Essays. New York: Columbia U P, 1956.

92 SENIOR, Nassau W. *Essays on Fiction.* London: Longman, Green, Longman, Roberts & Green, 1864. (Long studies of Scott, Bulwer-Lytton, Thackeray.)

93 SHAPIRO, Charles, ed. *Twelve Original Essays on Great English Novels.* Detroit: Wayne State U P, 1960.†

94 SIMON, Irène. *Formes du roman anglais de Dickens à Joyce.* Liège: Bibliothèque de la faculté de Philosophie et Lettres de l'Université de Liège, 1949–1951.

95 STANG, Richard. *The Theory of the Novel in England, 1850–1870.* New York: Columbia U P, 1959. (Study, with extensive quotation, of critical ideas.)*

96 TILLOTSON, Geoffrey. *Criticism and the Nineteenth Century.* London: Athlone, 1951.

97 TILLOTSON, Kathleen. *Novels of the Eighteen-Forties.* Oxford: Clarendon P, 1954.*†

98 VAN GHENT, Dorothy. *The English Novel: Form and Function.* New York: Rinehart, 1953.*†

99 VERSCHOYLE, Derek, ed. *The English Novelists.* London: Chatto & Windus, 1936. (Essays by modern English novelists.)

100 WELSH, Alexander. "The Allegory of Truth in Victorian Fiction." *VS*, 9(1967):7–28.

101 WRIGHT, Austin, ed. *Victorian Literature: Modern Essays in Criticism.* New York: Oxford U P, 1961.†

Special Topics

Historical, Social, and Intellectual Background

102 APPLEMAN, Philip, et al., eds. *1859: Entering an Age of Crisis*. Bloomington: Indiana U P, 1959.

103 BRIGGS, Asa. *The Age of Improvement, 1783-1867*. London, New York: Longmans, Green, 1958. [Paperback title, *Making of Modern England 1783-1867*.]*†

104 BRIGGS, Asa. *Victorian Cities*. London: Odhams, 1963.

105 BRIGGS, Asa. *Victorian People*. London: Odhams, 1954.†

106 BROWN, Alan. *The Metaphysical Society, Victorian Minds in Crisis, 1869-1880*. New York: Columbia U P, 1947.

107 BUCKLEY, Jerome H. *The Victorian Temper*. Cambridge, Mass.: Harvard U P, 1951.†

108 BURN, W. L. *The Age of Equipoise*. London: Allen & Unwin, 1964.†

109 CLARK, G. Kitson. *The Making of Victorian England*. Cambridge, Mass.: Harvard U P, 1962.

110 COCKSHUT, A. O. J. *The Unbelievers*. London: Collins, 1964.

111 DECKER, Clarence R. *The Victorian Conscience*. New York: Twayne, 1952.

112 DODDS, John W. *The Age of Paradox. A Biography of England: 1841-1851*. London: Gollancz, 1953.

113 ENGELS, Friederich. *The Condition of the Working Class in England in 1844*. Trans. and ed. W. O. Henderson and W. H. Chaloner. London: Blackwell, 1958.

114 GREENBERGER, Allen J. *The British Image of India: A Study in the Literature of Imperialism*. Oxford: Oxford U P, 1969.

115 HALÉVY, E. *History of the English People in the Nineteenth Century*. Trans. E. I. Watkin. 6 vols. 2d ed., New York: Barnes & Noble, 1949-1952.†

116 HIMMELFARB, G. *Victorian Minds*. New York: Knopf, 1968.†

117 HOLLOWAY, John. *The Victorian Sage*. London: Macmillan, 1953. (Includes studies of Disraeli, George Eliot, Newman, Hardy.)*†

118 HOUGHTON, Walter E. *The Victorian Frame of Mind, 1830-1870*. New Haven: Yale U P, 1957.*†

119 HOWARD, David B., et al., eds. *Tradition and Tolerance in Nineteenth-Century Fiction*. New York: Barnes & Noble, 1967.

120   LAVER, James D. *The Age of Optimism: Manners and Morals, 1848–1914.* London: Weidenfeld & Nicholson, 1966. (Pub. as *Manners and Morals in the Age of Optimism, 1848–1914.* New York: Harper & Row, 1966.)

121   MARCUS, Steven. *The Other Victorians: A Study of Sexuality and Pornography in Mid-Nineteenth Century England.* New York: Basic Books, 1966.†

122   MAYHEW, Henry. *London Labour and the London Poor.* 3 vols, 1861; 4 vols, London: Griffin, 1862. *Selections from London Labour and the London Poor.* WC. Ed. John L. Bradley. Oxford: Oxford U P, 1965.*

123   MILLER, J. Hillis. *The Disappearance of God.* Cambridge, Mass.: Belknap of Harvard U P, 1963.*†

124   MOERS, Ellen. *The Dandy: Brummell to Beerbohm.* New York: Viking, 1960.

125   NEFF, Emery. *Carlyle and Mill: An Introduction to Victorian Thought.* New York: Columbia U P, 1926.

126   PECKHAM, Morse. *Beyond the Tragic Vision: The Quest for Identity in the Nineteenth Century.* New York: Braziller, 1962.

127   RALEIGH, John H. "Victorian Morals and the Modern Novel." *PR,* 31(1958):241–64. Repr. *Time, Place, and Idea.* Carbondale: Southern Illinois U P, 1968, pp. 137–63.*

128   REED, John R. *Old School Ties: The Public Schools in British Literature.* Syracuse: Syracuse U P, 1965. (Begins with Victorians and Dickens.)

129   SCHNEIDER, R. M. "Loss and Gain? The Theme of Conversion in Late Victorian Fiction." *VS,* 9(1965):29–44.

130   SOMERVELL, D. C. *English Thought in the Nineteenth Century.* London: Methuen, 1929.†

131   STRACHEY, Lytton. *Eminent Victorians.* London: Chatto & Windus, 1918.*†

132   SUSSMAN, Herbert L. *Victorians and the Machine: The Literary Response to Technology.* Cambridge, Mass.: Harvard U P, 1968.

133   THOMSON, David. *England in the Nineteenth Century (1815–1914).* Harmondsworth, Middlesex: Penguin, 1950.†

134   WILLEY, Basil. *More Nineteenth Century Studies: A Group of Honest Doubters.* London: Chatto & Windus, 1956. (Includes study of "Mark Rutherford.")*

135   WILLEY, Basil. *Nineteenth Century Studies.* London: Chatto & Windus, 1949. (Includes studies of Newman and George Eliot.)*

136   WILLIAMS, Raymond. *Culture and Society: 1780–1950.* New York: Columbia U P, 1958.*†

137   WOODWARD, E. L. *The Age of Reform 1815–1850.* Oxford: Clarendon P, 1938. [The Oxford History of England, 1934–   .]

138   YOUNG, G. M. *Victorian England: Portrait of an Age.* New York: Oxford U P, 1953.*†

139   YOUNG, G. M., ed. *Early Victorian England.* 2 vols. Oxford: Clarendon P, 1934. (Surveys by specialists of many aspects of Victorian life.)*

Publishing, Authorship, and the Reading Public

140 ALTICK, Richard D. *The English Common Reader, 1800-1900.* Chicago: U of Chicago P, 1957.*† (For a fuller bibliography, see 6, Vol. III, columns 25-90, 1755-1884.)

141 ALTICK, Richard D. "Nineteenth-Century English Best-Sellers: A Further List." *SB,* 22(1969):197-206.

142 BALD, Marjory A. *Women Writers of the Nineteenth Century.* Cambridge: Cambridge U P, 1923.

143 Ballantyne & Company. *The History of the Ballantyne Press and Its Connexion with Sir Walter Scott, Bart.* Edinburgh: Ballantyne, Hanson, 1871.

144 COLBY, Vineta and Robert A. *The Equivocal Virtue: Mrs. Oliphant and the Victorian Literary Market Place.* Hamden, Conn.: Shoe String P, 1966.

145 COX, Harold, and J. E. CHANDLER. *The House of Longman, 1724-1924. With a Record of Their Bicentenary Celebrations.* London: Longmans, Green, 1925. (Printed for private circulation.)

146 CRUSE, Amy. *The Victorians and Their Books.* London: Allen & Unwin, 1935.

147 DALZIEL, Margaret. *Popular Fiction a Hundred Years Ago.* London: Cohen & West, 1957.

148 GETTMANN, Royal A. *A Victorian Publisher.* Cambridge: Cambridge U P, 1960. (Richard Bentley.)

149 GRIEST, Guinevere L. "A Victorian Leviathan: Mudie's Select Library." *NCF,* 20(1965):103-26.

150 GROSS, John. *The Rise and Fall of the Man of Letters: English Literary Life since 1800.* London: Weidenfeld & Nicolson, 1969.*

151 HAINING, Peter, ed. *The Gentlewomen of Evil; An Anthology of Rare Supernatural Stories from the Pens of Victorian Ladies.* New York: Taplinger, 1967. (George Eliot, Mary Shelley, Catherine Crowe, Mrs. Oliphant, Mrs. Gaskell, Mrs. Henry Wood, Miss Braddon, and Mrs. Molesworth.)

152 HARRISON, Sir Cecil Reeves and Harry George. *The House of Harrison: Being an Account of the Family and Firm of Harrison & Sons, Printers to the King.* London: Harrison, 1914.

153 HINKLEY, Laura L. *Ladies of Literature.* New York: Hastings, 1946.

154 JAMES, Louis. *Fiction for the Working Man, 1830-1850.* New York: Oxford U P, 1963.*

155 KEITH, Sarah. "Mudie's Circulating Library." *NCF,* 11(1956):156-7. (Report on the author's compilation of a list of some 3,000 titles circulated by Mudie's in the 1840's, 1850's, and 1860's.)

156 LEAVIS, Queenie D. *Fiction and the Reading Public.* London: Chatto & Windus, 1932, 1965.*

157 MASEFIELD, Muriel. *Women Novelists from Fanny Burney to George Eliot.* London: Nicholson & Watson, 1934.

158 MAXWELL, Christabel. *Mrs. Gatty and Mrs. Ewing.* London: Constable, 1949. (Mother and daughter; popular writers mainly for children.)

159 MORGAN, Charles. *The House of Macmillan, 1843-1943.* London: Macmillan, 1944.

160 MUMBY, F. A. *The House of Routledge, 1834-1934: With a History of Kegan Paul, Trench, Trübner and Other Associate Firms.* London: Routledge, 1934.

161 SADLEIR, Michael. "The Camel's Back, or the Last Tribulation of a Victorian Publisher." *Essays Mainly on the Nineteenth Century Presented to Sir Humphrey Milford.* London and New York: Oxford U P, 1948. (On the publisher George Bentley and the late Victorian popular novelist Marie Corelli.)

162 STEBBINS, Lucy Poate. *A Victorian Album: Some Lady Novelists of the Period.* New York: Columbia U P, 1946.

163 THOMPSON, E. P. *The Making of the English Working Class.* London: Gollancz, 1963. (Much on working class reading and writing in early nineteenth century.)*

164 WALBANK, Felix A., ed. *Queens of the Circulating Library: Selections from Victorian Lady Novelists, 1850-1900.* London: Evans, 1950.

165 WAUGH, Arthur. *A Hundred Years of Publishing, being the Story of Chapman and Hall, Ltd.* London: Chapman & Hall, 1930.

Genres, Schools, Influences, and Subjects

166 BAILEY, James O. *Pilgrims through Space and Time.* New York: Argus, 1947. (A study of science- and utopian fiction.)

167 BAKER, Joseph E. *The Novel and the Oxford Movement.* Princeton: Princeton U P, 1932.

168 BENTLEY, Phyllis. *The English Regional Novel.* London: Allen & Unwin, 1942.

169 BRAMLEY, J. A. "Religion and the Novelists." *CR*, 180(1951):348-53.

170 CAZAMIAN, Louis. *Le roman social en Angleterre, 1830-1850.* Paris: Société d'édition, 1904.

171 CAZAMIAN, Madeleine L. *Le roman et les idées en Angleterre.* 3 parts. London and New York: Oxford U P, 1923-1955. *L'Influence de la science, 1860-1890,* (1923); *L'Anti-intellectualisme et l'esthétisme, 1880-1900,* (1935); *Les doctrines d'action et l'aventure, 1880-1914,* (1955)*

172 COVENY, Peter. *Poor Monkey: The Child in Literature.* London: Rockliff, 1957. [Rev. ed. 1967, Penguin, as *The Image of Childhood.*]†

173 CRAIG, David. *Scottish Literature and the Scottish People: 1680-1830.* London: Chatto and Windus, 1961.*

174 CRAIG, G. Armour. "The Unpoetic Compromise: On the Relation between Private Vision and Social Order in Nineteenth-Century English Fiction." In 91.*

175 DEVONSHIRE, Marian Gladys. *The English Novel in France, 1830-1870.* London: U of London P, 1929.

176 DRUMMOND, Andrew L. *The Churches in English Fiction.* Leicester: Backus, 1950.

177 ELLIS, S. M. *Wilkie Collins, Le Fanu and Others.* London: Constable, 1931. (On the "sensational novel.")

178 FRIERSON, W. C. *L'Influence du naturalisme français sur les romanciers anglais de 1885 à 1900.* Paris: Giard, 1925.

179 GARRETT, Peter K. *Scene and Symbol from George Eliot to James Joyce: Studies in Changing Fictional Mode.* YSE 172. New Haven: Yale U P, 1969.

180 HARRIS, Wendell V. "English Short Fiction in the Nineteenth Century." *SSF*, 6(1968):1-93.

181 HAYCRAFT, Howard. *Murder for Pleasure: The Life and Times of the Detective Story.* New York: Appleton-Century-Crofts, 1941. (On English and American detective fiction from 1841 on.)

182 HENKIN, Leo J. *Darwinism in the English Novel, 1860-1910.* New York: Corporate, 1940.

183 HOLLINGSWORTH, Keith. *The Newgate Novel, 1830-1847.* Detroit: Wayne State U P, 1963.

184 HOWE, Susanne. *Novels of Empire.* New York: Columbia U P, 1949. (Treats literature of colonization.)

185 HOWE, Susanne. *Wilhelm Meister and His English Kinsmen.* New York: Columbia U P, 1950. (Studies German influence on English fiction.)

186 KEMPTON, Kenneth P. *The Short Story.* Cambridge, Mass.: Harvard U P, 1967.

187 KNOEPFLMACHER, U. C. *Religious Humanism and the Victorian Novel: George Eliot, Walter Pater, and Samuel Butler.* Princeton: Princeton U P, 1965.*

188 KRANS, Horatio S. *Irish Life in Irish Fiction.* New York: Columbia U P, 1903.

189 LASKI, Marghanita. *Mrs. Ewing, Mrs. Molesworth, and Mrs. Hodgson Burnett.* London: Barker, 1950. (With lists of the works of three of the most famous Victorian writers of children's fiction.)

190 LUKÁCS, Georg. *The Historical Novel.* Boston: Beacon, 1963.*†

191 MADDEN, William A. "The Search for Forgiveness in Some Nineteenth-Century English Novels." *CLS*, 3(1966) 139-53. (Includes *The Heart of Midlothian, Vanity Fair, Wuthering Heights, Middlemarch, Tess of the d'Urbervilles.*)

192 MAISON, Margaret. *Search Your Soul, Eustace; A Survey of the Religious Novel in the Victorian Age.* London: Sheed & Ward, 1961. [New York: Sheed & Ward, 1962, as *The Victorian Vision: Studies in the Religious Novel.*] (Inferior to 167.)

12   SPECIAL TOPICS

193 MARANDON, Sylvaine. *L'image de la France dans l'Angleterre victorienne 1848-1900.* Paris: Colin, 1967.

194 MARRIOTT, Sir John. *English History in English Fiction.* New York: Dutton, 1941.

195 MARTIN, Hazel T. *Petticoat Rebels: A Study of the Novels of Social Protest of George Eliot, Elizabeth Gaskell, and Charlotte Brontë.* New York: Helios, 1968.

196 MUIR, Percival Horace. *English Children's Books, 1600 to 1900.* London: Batsford, 1954.

197 MURCH, A. E. *The Development of the Detective Novel.* London: Owen, 1958.

198 PENZOLDT, Peter. *The Supernatural in Fiction.* London: Nevill, 1952. (Illuminating, though limited to short stories.)

199 PHELPS, Gilbert. *The Russian Novel in English Fiction.* London: Hutchinson, 1956.

200 PHILLIPS, Walter C. *Dickens, Reade, and Collins—Sensation Novelists.* New York: Columbia U P, 1919.

201 PRAZ, Mario. *The Hero in Eclipse in Victorian Fiction.* Trans. Angus Davidson. New York: Oxford U P, 1956.*†

202 PROCTOR, Mortimer R. *The English University Novel.* Berkeley and Los Angeles: U of California P, 1957. (Chapters IV to VIII mainly devoted to nineteenth century. Bibliography.)

203 REID, Forrest. "Minor Fiction in the 'Eighties.'" In 36.

204 ROSA, Matthew Whiting. *The Silver Fork School.* New York: Columbia U P, 1936.

205 ROSENBERG, Edgar. *From Shylock to Svengali: Jewish Stereotypes in English Fiction.* Stanford: Stanford U P, 1960. (Contains chapters on Scott, Dickens, Trollope, Bulwer-Lytton, George Eliot.)*

206 RUSSELL, Frances Theresa. *Satire in the Victorian Novel.* New York: Macmillan, 1920.

207 SCHNEIDER, R. M. "Loss and Gain? The Theme of Conversion in Late Victorian Fiction." See 129.

208 SCHUBEL, Friedrich. *Die "Fashionable Novels," ein Kapital zur englischen Kultur und Romangeschichte.* Uppsala: Lundquist; Cambridge, Mass.: Harvard U P, 1952.

209 SINGH, Bhupal. *A Survey of Anglo-Indian Fiction.* London: Oxford U P, 1934. (Chapter on "Meadows Taylor and the Predecessors of Kipling." Bibliography.)

210 SPEARE, Morris E. *The Political Novel: Its Development in England and America.* New York: Oxford U P, 1924.

211 THOMSON, Patricia. *The Victorian Heroine: A Changing Ideal.* London and New York: Oxford U P, 1956.

212 UTTER, Robert P., and Gwendolyn B. NEEDHAM. *Pamela's Daughters.* New York: Macmillan, 1936. (Examines role of the heroine in popular novels.)

213 WILLIAMS, Raymond. *The English Novel from Dickens to Lawrence.* New York: Oxford U P, 1970.*

214 WILSON, Mona. *These Were Muses.* London: Sidgwick & Jackson, 1924. (Popular studies of literary women, including Sydney Morgan, Jane Porter, and Frances Trollope.)

Individual Novelists

Ainsworth, William Harrison (1805–1882)

MAIN NOVELS

215 *Rookwood. A Romance.* 3 vols., 1834–1836. *Crichton.* 3 vols., 1837. (Rev. ed. 1849.) *Jack Sheppard. A Romance,* 1839. (First pub. in *Bentley's Misc.,* 1839–1840.) *The Tower of London,* 1840. (In 13 monthly parts, 1840.) *Old St. Paul's. A Tale of the Plague and the Fire,* 1841. (First pub. in *Sunday Times,* Jan-Dec. 1841.) *The Lancashire Witches. A Novel.* 3 vols., 1849. (First pub. in *Sunday Times,* 1848.)

STUDIES

See 62.

215A ELLIS, S. M. *William Harrison Ainsworth and His Friends.* 2 vols. London: Lane, 1911.

Allen, Grant (Charles Grant Blairfindie Allen), (1848–1899)

MAIN NOVELS

216 *The Woman Who Did,* 1895. *The British Barbarians: A Hill-Top Novel,* 1895.

STUDIES

See 61.

Banim, John (1798–1842) and Michael (1796–1874)

MAIN NOVELS (usually under pseudonym "The O'Hara Family")

217 *Tales by the O'Hara Family.* Series 1, 3 vols., 1825; Ser. 2, 3 vols., 1826. *The Boyne Water.* 3 vols. 1828. (By John Banim.) *The Smuggler.* 3 vols., 1830. (By John Banim.) *The Ghost-Hunter and His Family,* 1833. (By Michael Banim.) *Father Connell.* 3 vols., 1842.

STUDIES

See Flanagan, 38,* 188.

218 MURRAY, P. J. *The Life of John Banim.* London: Lay, 1857.

219 STEGER, M. A. *John Banim, ein Nachahmer Walter Scotts.* Erlangen: 1935. (Doctoral dissertation.)

Baring-Gould, Sabine (1834–1924)

MAIN NOVELS

220 *Mehala. A Story of the Salt Marshes.* 2 vols., 1880. *Red Spider.* 2 vols., 1887. *The Gaverocks. A Tale of the Cornish Coast.* 3 vols., 1887. *Cheap Jack Zita.* 3 vols., 1893.

STUDIES

221 BARING-GOULD, Sabine. *Early Reminiscences 1834–1864.* London: Lane Bodley Head, 1923. Repr. Detroit: Gale, 1968,

222 BARING-GOULD, Sabine. *Further Reminiscences 1864–1894.* New York: Dutton, 1925. Repr. Detroit: Gale, 1968.

223 FOWLES, John. Introduction to *Mehalah.* London: Chatto & Windus, 1969.

224 HYDE, William J. "The Stature of Baring-Gould as a Novelist." *NCF,* 15(1960):1–6.

Besant, Walter (1836–1901)

MAIN NOVELS

225 *Ready-Money Mortiboy.* 3 vols., 1872. (With James Rice.) *The Golden Butterfly.* 3 vols., 1876. (With James Rice.) *The Chaplain of the Fleet.* 3 vols., 1881. (With James Rice.) *All Sorts and Conditions of Men.* 3 vols., 1882. *Dorothy Forster.* 3 vols., 1884. *Children of Gibeon.* 3 vols., 1886. *The World Went Very Well Then.* 3 vols., 1887. *Beyond the Dreams of Avarice,* 1895.

STUDIES

See 65.

226 BESANT, Walter. *Autobiography.* 1902.

227 BOEGE, F. W. "Sir Walter Besant, Novelist." *NCF,* 10(1956):248-80; 11(1956):32-60.

Blackmore, Richard Doddridge (1825-1900)

MAIN NOVELS

228 *Lorna Doone. A Romance of Exmoor.* 3 vols., 1869. *The Maid of Sker.* 3 vols., 1872. *Alice Lorraine. A Tale of the South Downs.* 3 vols., 1875. *Cripps the Carrier. A Woodland Tale.* 3 vols., 1876. *Springhaven. A Tale of the Great War.* 3 vols., 1887.

STUDIES

See 62.

229 *Blackmore Studies, I* (1969). (Kenneth Budd, "*Lorna Doone:* A 'Christian Novel,' " 2; Nikolai Tolstoy, "Plover's Barrows Identified," 3; "The Old Gate at Blundell's," 5; Nikolai Tolstoy, "The Location of 'Glen Doone,' " 6-8; John Yeowell, "Appetites and Victuals at Plover's Barrows," 9-11; "Blackmore Bibliography," 11.)

230 BUDD, Kenneth. *The Last Victorian: R. D. Blackmore and His Novels.* London: Centaur, 1960.

231 BURRIS, Quincy G. *Richard Doddridge Blackmore, His Life and Novels.* Illinois Studies in Language and Literature No. 15. Urbana: U of Illinois P, 1930. (Contains bibliography.)

232 DUNN, W. H. *R. D. Blackmore: The Author of* Lorna Doone. New York: Longmans, Green, 1956. (Contains bibliography.)

Blessington, Marguerite, Countess of, née Power (1789-1849)

MAIN NOVELS

233 *The Repealers.* 3 vols., 1833. *The Two Friends.* 3 vols., 1835. *The Victims of Society.* 3 vols., 1837. *The Governess.* 2 vols., 1839.

STUDIES

234 MADDEN, R. R. *The Literary Life and Correspondence of the Countess of Blessington.* 3 vols. London, 1855.

235 SADLEIR, Michael. *Blessington-D'Orsay: A Masquerade.* London: Constable, 1933.

Borrow, George Henry (1803–1881)

NOVELS

236   *Lavengro.* 3 vols. London: Murray, 1851. *The Romany Rye.* 2 vols. London: Murray, 1857.

BIBLIOGRAPHY, COLLECTED EDITIONS, BIOGRAPHY, AND CRITICISM

237   WISE, T. J. *A Bibliography of the Writings in Prose and Verse of George Henry Borrow.* London: Clay, 1914.

238   *The Works of George Borrow.* Norwich Edition. Ed. Clement Shorter. 16 vols. London: Constable; New York: Wells, 1923–1924.

239   ARMSTRONG, Martin. *George Borrow.* London: Barker, 1950.*

240   FRÉCHET, René. "George Borrow devant la critique." *EA*, 7(1954):257–70.

241   FRÉCHET, René. *George Borrow (1803–1881), vagabond, polyglotte, agent biblique, écrivain.* Paris: Didier, 1956.

242   KNAPP, William Ireland. *The Life, Writings and Correspondence of George Borrow.* 2 vols. New York: Putnam, 1899. Repr., Detroit: Gale, 1968.

243   MEYERS, Robert R. *George Borrow.* New York: Twayne, 1966.

244   PEARSALL, Ronald. "A Corner in Gipsies." *QR*, 305(1967):189–95.

245   SHORTER, Clement. *The Life of George Borrow.* New York: Dutton, 1928. (First pub. in 1913 as *Borrow and His Circle.*)

246   TILFORD, John E., Jr. "Contemporary Criticism of *Lavengro:* a Re-examination." *SP*, 41(1944):442–56.

247   TILFORD, John E., Jr. "The Critical Approach to *Lavengro-Romany Rye.*" *SP*, 46(1949):79–96.

248   TILFORD, John E., Jr. "The Formal Artistry of *Lavengro-Romany Rye.*" *PMLA*, 44(1949):369–84.

Braddon, Mary Elizabeth, Later Maxwell (1837–1915)

MAIN NOVELS

249   *Lady Audley's Secret.* 3 vols., 1862. *Aurora Floyd.* 3 vols., 1863. *John Marchmont's Legacy.* 3 vols., 1863. *Dead Men's Shoes.* 3 vols., 1876. *Vixen: A Novel.* 3 vols., 1879. *London Pride, or When the World Was Younger,* 1896.

STUDIES

See 1754.*

250 HEYWOOD, C. "Flaubert, Miss Braddon, and George Moore." *CL*, 12(1960):151–8. [See also: *RLC*, 38(1964):255–61.]

251 SADLEIR, Michael. "Notes on *Lady Audley's Secret.*" *TLS*, May 11, 1940.

The Brontës

Treated collectively (as they too often are).

BIBLIOGRAPHY AND REFERENCE

See 25.*

252 *Transactions of the Brontë Society.* 1895-   . (Contains many bibliographical and biographical records. Abbreviated *BST.*)

253 "Brontë Society Publications 1865-1965." *BST*, 15(1966):96–102. (Bibliography of monographs and essays pub. in *BST.*)

254 WISE, Thomas James. *A Bibliography of the Writings in Prose and Verse of the Members of the Brontë Family.* London: Clay, 1917. [Printed for private circulation only.].

TEXTS

255 *Life and Works of Charlotte Brontë and Her Sisters.* Ed., with prefaces by Mrs. Humphry Ward, and Mrs. Gaskell's *Life of Charlotte Brontë;* annotated by Clement Shorter. 7 vols. London: Smith, Elder, 1899-1900. (The Haworth Edition.)

256 *The Shakespeare Head Brontë.* 19 vols. Ed. T. J. Wise and J. A. Symington. Oxford: Shakespeare Head, 1931-1938. (Includes, besides the novels, lives, letters, published and unpublished miscellaneous writings.)*

BIOGRAPHICAL AND CRITICAL

See 52 (on Charlotte and Emily.)*

257 BENTLEY, Phyllis. *The Brontë Sisters* (1950). WTW. Rev. ed. London and New York: Longmans, Green, 1950.

258 BENTLEY, Phyllis. *The Brontës and Their World.* New York: Viking, 1969. (Illustrated.)

259 CHASE, Richard. "The Brontës." *KR*, 9(1947):487–506.

260 CRAIK, Wendy A. *The Brontë Novels.* London: Methuen, 1968.

261 DELAFIELD, E. M. [pseud.], ed. *The Brontës: Their Lives Recorded by Their Contemporaries.* London: Hogarth, 1935.

262 DU MAURIER, Daphne. *The Infernal World of Branwell Brontë.* Garden City, N.Y.: Doubleday, 1960.†

263 EWBANK, Inga Stina. *Their Proper Sphere: A Study of the Brontë Sisters as Early Victorian Novelists.* Cambridge, Mass.: Harvard U P, 1966.*

264 GÉRIN, Winifred. *Branwell Brontë.* London and New York: Nelson, 1961.

265 GÉRIN, Winifred. *Charlotte Brontë: The Evolution of Genius.* Oxford: Clarendon P, 1967.*†

266 HANSON, Lawrence, and Elizabeth M. HANSON. *The Four Brontës.* London and New York: Oxford U P, 1949.

267 HARRISON, Grace E. *Haworth Parsonage; A Study of Wesley and the Brontës.* London: Epworth, 1948. (On the Evangelical influence.)

268 HINKLEY, Laura L. *The Brontës, Charlotte and Emily.* New York: Hastings, 1945.*

269 HOPKINS, A. B. *The Father of the Brontës.* Baltimore: Johns Hopkins U P, 1958.

270 KINSLEY, E. E. *Pattern for Genius: A Story of Branwell Brontë and His Three Sisters.* New York: Dutton, 1939.

271 LANE, Margaret. *The Brontë Story: A Reconsideration of Mrs. Gaskell's Life of Charlotte Brontë.* London: Heinemann, 1948.*

272 O'NEILL, Judith. *Critics on Charlotte and Emily Brontë.* RLitC. Coral Gables, Fla.: U of Miami P, 1969.

273 RATCHFORD, Fannie E. *The Brontës' Web of Childhood.* New York: Columbia U P, 1941.*

274 READ, Sir Herbert. "Charlotte and Emily Brontë." *YR,* 14(1925):720–38.

275 SHORTER, Clement, ed. *The Brontës: Life and Letters.* 2 vols. New York: Scribner's, 1908.

276 SHORTER, Clement. *Charlotte Brontë and Her Circle.* London, 1896. (Repub. as *Charlotte Brontë and Her Sisters* [1905]; and rev. as *The Brontës and Their Circle* [1914].)

277 SINCLAIR, May. *The Three Brontës.* Boston and New York: Houghton Mifflin, 1912.

278 SUGDEN, K. A. R. *A Short History of the Brontës.* London: Oxford U P, 1929.

279 WATSON, Melvin R. "Form and Substance in the Brontë Novels," In 88, pp. 106–17.*

280 WEIR, Edith M. "Contemporary Reviews of the First Brontë Novels." *BST,* 11,ii(1947):89–96.

281 WEST, Rebecca. "The Role of Fantasy in the Work of the Brontës." *BST,* 12,iv(1954):255–67.

282 WILLIS, Irene Cooper. *The Brontës.* London: Duckworth, 1934.

283 WISE, Thomas J., and J. A. SYMINGTON. *The Brontës: Their Lives, Friendships and Correspondence.* In 256, 4 vols.*

Brontë, Anne ("Acton Bell") (1820–1849)

NOVELS

284 *Agnes Grey.* London: Newby, 1847. *The Tenant of Wildfell Hall.* 3 vols. London: Newby, 1848.

BIOGRAPHICAL AND CRITICAL

285 BELL, A. Craig. "Anne Brontë: A Re-Appraisal." *QR*, 304(1966):315–21.

286 GÉRIN, Winifred. *Anne Brontë: A Biography.* London and New York: Nelson, 1959.

287 HALE, Will T. "Anne Brontë: Her Life and Writings." *Indiana U Studies*, 16, xxciii(1929):3–44.

288 HARRISON, Ada, and Derek STANFORD. *Anne Brontë: Her Life and Work.* London: Methuen, 1959.

289 STEVENSON, W. H. *Emily and Anne Brontë.* New York: Humanities P, 1968.†

Brontë, Charlotte, Later Nicholls ("Currer Bell") (1816–1855)

NOVELS

290 Jane Eyre. 3 vols. London: Smith, Elder, 1847. *Shirley.* 3 vols. London: Smith, Elder, 1849. *Villette.* 3 vols. London: Smith, Elder, 1853. *The Professor.* 2 vols. London: Smith, Elder, 1857.

BIBLIOGRAPHY

291 HATFIELD, C. W. "The Early Manuscripts of Charlotte Brontë." *BST*, 6(1922):97–111; (1923):153–65; (1924):220–35.

BIOGRAPHICAL AND GENERAL

292 BENSON, E. F. *Charlotte Brontë.* London and New York: Longmans, Green, 1932.

293 CROMPTON, Margaret. *Passionate Search: A Life of Charlotte Brontë.* New York: McKay, 1956.

294 DOOLEY, Lucille. "Psycho-Analysis of Charlotte Brontë as a Type of the Woman of Genius." *American Journal of Psychology*, 31(1920):221–72.

295 GASKELL, Elizabeth Cleghorn. *Letters on Charlotte Brontë by Mrs. Gaskell.* Ed. Clement Shorter. London, 1915. (Printed for private circulation.)

296 GASKELL, Elizabeth Cleghorn. *The Life of Charlotte Brontë.* 2 vols., 3 eds. London: Smith, Elder, 1857. (Passages suppressed from this work may be found in *BST*, 6(1921):50–65.)*

297 POLLARD, Arthur. *Charlotte Brontë.* New York: Humanities, 1967.†

CRITICAL

298 DRY, Florence S. "The Sources of *Jane Eyre*." In 368.

299 HEILMAN, Robert B. "Charlotte Brontë, Reason, and the Moon." *NCF*, 14(1960):283-392.

300 HEILMAN, Robert B. "Charlotte Bronte's 'New' Gothic." In 88, pp. 118-32.*

301 KNIES, Earl A. "The Artistry of Charlotte Brontë, A Reassessment." *OUR*, 7(1965):21-39.

302 MARTIN, Robert B. *The Accents of Persuasion: Charlotte Bronte's Novels.* London: Faber, 1966.

303 MOMBERGER, Philip. "Self and World in the Works of Charlotte Brontë." *ELH*, 32(1965):349-69.

304 SPENS, J. "Charlotte Brontë." *E&S*, 14(1928):54-70.

305 SWINBURNE, Algernon Charles. *A Note on Charlotte Brontë.* London: Chatto & Windus, 1877.

306 WEST, Rebecca. "Charlotte Brontë." In 79.

307 WROOT, H. E. "Sources of Charlotte Brontë's Novels: Persons and Places." *BST*, Supp. to 8(1935).

JANE EYRE

308 *Jane Eyre*. Eds. Jane Jack and Margaret Smith. Oxford: Clarendon P, 1969. (Critical text with explanatory notes and appendices. First vol. in the Clarendon Edition of the novels of the Brontës, under the general editorship of Ian and Jane Jack.)*

309 GRIBBLE, Jennifer. "Jane Eyre's Imagination." *NCF*, 23(1968):279-93.

310 HUGHES, R. E. "*Jane Eyre:* The Unbaptized Dionysos." *NCF*, 18(1964):347-64.

311 KNIES, Earl A. "The 'I' of Jane Eyre." *CE*, 27(1966):546-8, 553-6.

312 LODGE, David. "Fire and Eyre: Charlotte Brontë's War of Earthly Elements." In his 74, pp. 114-43.

313 MARSHALL, William H. "The Self, the World, and the Structure of *Jane Eyre*." *RLV*, 27(1961):416-25.

314 MOSER, Lawrence E., S. J. "From Portrait to Person: A Note on the Surrealistic in *Jane Eyre*." *NCF*, 20(1965):275-81.

315 PRESCOTT, Joseph. "*Jane Eyre:* A Romantic Exemplum with a Difference." In 93, pp. 87-102. Also in *SEL*, 20(1959):1-13.

316 SCARGILL, M. H. "All Passion Spent: A Revaluation of *Jane Eyre*." *UTQ*, 19(1950):120-5.

317 SHANNON, Edgar F., Jr. "The Present Tense in *Jane Eyre*." *NCF*, 10(1955):141-5.

318 SHAPIRO, Arnold. "In Defense of Jane Eyre." *SEL*, 8 (1968):681-98.

319 SOLOMON, Eric. "*Jane Eyre*: Fire and Water." *CE*, 25(1963):215-7.

320 TILLOTSON, Kathleen. In 97, pp. 286-313.*

321 WOOLF, Virginia. "*Jane Eyre* and *Wuthering Heights.*" *The Common Reader: First Series* [1925]. London: Penguin, 1938, pp. 154-60.†

SHIRLEY

322 BRIGGS, Asa. "Private and Social Themes in *Shirley.*" *BST*, 13(1958):203-19.

323 GIRDLER, Lew. "Charlotte Brontë's *Shirley* and Scott's *The Black Dwarf.*" *MLN*, 71(1956):187.

324 HOLGATE, Ivy. "The Structure of *Shirley.*" *BST*, 4(1962):27-35.

325 KNIES, Earl A. "Art, Death, and the Composition of *Shirley.*" *VN*, 28(1965):22-4.

326 KORG, Jacob. "The Problem of Unity in *Shirley.*" *NCF*, 12(1957):125-36.

327 SHAPIRO, Arnold. "Public Themes and Private Lives: Social Criticism in *Shirley.*" *PLL*, 4(1968):74-84.

328 TOMPKINS, J. M. S. "Caroline Helstone's Eyes." *BST*, 14(1961):18-28.

VILLETTE

329 COLBY, Robert A. "*Villette* and the Life of the Mind." *PMLA*, 75(1960):410-9.

330 DUNBAR, Georgia S. "Proper Names in *Villette.*" *NCF*, 15(1960):77-80.

331 FALCONER, J. A. "*The Professor* and *Villette:* A Study of Development." *NCF*, 12(1957):125-36.

332 JOHNSON, E. D. H. " 'Daring the Dread Glance': Charlotte Brontë's Treatment of the Supernatural in *Villette.*" *NCF*, 20(1966):325-36.

Brontë, Emily Jane ("Ellis Bell") (1818-1848)

NOVELS

333 *Wuthering Heights.* 3 vols. London: Newby, 1847.

BIOGRAPHICAL AND GENERAL

334 HEWISH, John. *Emily Brontë: A Critical and Biographical Study.* New York: St Martin's, 1969.

335 RATCHFORD, Fannie E., ed. *Gondal's Queen: A Novel in Verse by Emily Jane Brontë.* Arranged with introduction and notes. Austin: U of Texas P, 1955.†*

336 SIMPSON, Charles W. *Emily Brontë.* London: Country Life; New York: Scribner's, 1929.*

337 SPARK, Muriel, and Derek STANFORD. *Emily Brontë, Her Life and Work.* London: Owen, 1953; New York: London House & Maxwell, 1960.*

338 WILSON, Romer [pseud.]. *All Alone, The Life and Private History of Emily Jane Brontë.* New York: Boni, 1920. (One of the many psychological and psychoanalytic studies of Emily Brontë.)

CRITICAL

339 BATAILLE, Georges. "Emily Brontë et le mal." *Critique,* 67(1957):100–12.

340 BLONDEL, Jacques. *Emily Brontë: expérience spirituelle et création poétique.* Publications de la Faculté des Lettres de l'Université de Clermont, 2d ser., fac. Clermont-Ferrand: Presses Universitaires de France, 1956.

341 BRACCO, Edgar J. "Emily Brontë's Second Novel." *BST,* 15(1966):28–33.

342 BUCHEN, Irving H. "Emily Brontë and the Metaphysics of Childhood and Love." *NCF,* 22(1967):63–70.

343 LIVERMORE, Anne Lapraik. "Byron and Emily Brontë." *QR,* 300(1962):337–44.

344 MORGAN, Charles. "Emily Brontë." In 79, I, 79–94.

345 PEARSALL, Robert B. "The Presiding Tropes of Emily Brontë." *CE,* 27(1966):267–73.

346 SWINBURNE, Algernon Charles. "Emily Brontë." *Miscellanies.* London: Chatto & Windus, 1866.

WUTHERING HEIGHTS

See 48, 50,* 52,* 98,* 123, 142, 191, 259, 281, 321.

347 EVERITT, Alastair, comp. Wuthering Heights: *An Anthology of Criticism.* London: Cass, 1969.

348 MOSER, Thomas C., ed. Wuthering Heights: *Text, Sources, Criticism.* New York: Harcourt, Brace, 1962.†

349 SALE, William M., Jr., ed. Wuthering Heights: *An Authoritative Text with Essays in Criticism.* New York: Norton, 1963.†

350 VOGLER, Thomas A., ed. Wuthering Heights: *A Collection of Critical Essays.* TCI. Englewood Cliffs, N.J.: Prentice-Hall, 1968.†

351 LETTIS, Richard, and William E. MORRIS, eds. *A Wuthering Heights Handbook.* New York: Odyssey, 1961.

352 ADAMS, Ruth M. "*Wuthering Heights:* The Land East of Eden." *NCF,* 13(1958);58–62.

353 ALLOTT, Miriam. "*Wuthering Heights*: The Rejection of Heathcliff." *EIC,* 8(1958):27–47.

354 BELL, Vereen M. "*Wuthering Heights* and the Unforgiveable Sin." *NCF,* 17(1962):188–91.

355 BELL, Vereen M. "*Wuthering Heights* as *Epos.*" *CE,* 25(1963):199–200, 205–08.

356 BRADNER, Leicester. "The Growth of *Wuthering Heights.*" *PMLA,* 68(1933):129–46.

357 BRICK, Allan R. "Lewes' Review of *Wuthering Heights*." *NCF*, 14(1960):355-9.

358 BRICK, Allan R. "*Wuthering Heights:* Narrators, Audience, and Message." *CE*, 21(1959):80-6.

359 BUCHEN, Irving H. "Metaphysical and Social Evolution in *Wuthering Heights*." *VN*, 31(1967):15-20.

360 BUCKLER, William E. "Chapter VII of *Wuthering Heights:* A Key to Interpretation." *NCF*, 7(1952):51-5.

361 BUCKLEY, Vincent. "Passion and Control in *Wuthering Heights*." *SoR*, n.s. 1 (1964):5-23.

362 CLAY, Charles Travis. "Notes on the Chronology of *Wuthering Heights*." *BST*, 12(1952):88-99.

363 COLLINS, Clifford. "Theme and Conventions in *Wuthering Heights*." *The Critic*, 1(1947):43-50.

364 COTT, Jeremy. "Structures of Sound: The Last Sentence of *Wuthering Heights*." *TSLL*, 6(1964):280-9.

365 DAVIES, Cecil W. "A Reading of *Wuthering Heights*." *EIC*, 19(1969):254-72.

366 DEAN, Christopher. "Joseph's Speech in *Wuthering Heights*." *N&Q*, 7(1960):73-6.

367 DREW, Philip. "Charlotte Brontë as a Critic of *Wuthering Heights*." *NCF*, 18(1964):365-81.

368 DRY, Florence S. *The Sources of Wuthering Heights*. Cambridge: Heffer, 1937. (Mainly Scott's "The Black Dwarf.")

369 FORD, Boris. "*Wuthering Heights*." *Scrutiny*, 7(1939):375-89.

370 FRASER, John. "The Name of Action: Nelly Dean and *Wuthering Heights*." *NCF*, 20(1965):223-36.

371 GIRDLER, Lew. "*Wuthering Heights* and Shakespeare." *HLQ*, 19(1956):385-92.

372 GLECKNER, Robert F. "Time in *Wuthering Heights*." *Criticism*, 1(1959):328-38.

373 GOODRIDGE, Jonathan F. *Emily Brontë: "Wuthering Heights."* *SEngL*. London: Arnold, 1964.

374 GOSE, Elliot B., Jr. "*Wuthering Heights:* The Heath and the Hearth." *NCF*, 21(1966):1-19.

375 HAFLEY, James. "The Villain in *Wuthering Heights*." *NCF*, 13(1958):199-215. (Ellen Dean, "one of the most consummate villains in English literature.")

376 HAGAN, John H., Jr. "Control of Sympathy in *Wuthering Heights*." *NCF*, 21(1967):305-23.

377 JORDAN, John E. "The Ironic Vision of Emily Brontë." *NCF*, 20(1965):1-18.*

378 KAVANAGH, Colman. *The Symbolism of* Wuthering Heights. London: Long, 1920.

379 KLINGOPULOS, G. D. "*Wuthering Heights:* The Novel as Dramatic Poem, II." *Scrutiny,* 14(1947):269-86.

380 LAAR, Elizabeth Th. M. Van De. *The Inner Structure of* Wuthering Heights. *A Study of an Imaginative Field.* The Hague: Mouton, 1969.

381 LEHMAN, B. H. "Of Material, Subject, and Form: *Wuthering Heights.*" *The Image of the Work.* Berkeley: U of California P, 1955.

382 LEWIS, C. Day. "Emily Brontë." *Notable Images of Virtue.* Toronto: Ryerson, 1954.

383 LUCAS, Peter D. *An Introduction to the Psychology of* Wuthering Heights. London: Guild of Pastoral Psychology, 1943. (Guild Lectures.)

384 MARSDEN, Hilden. "The Scenic Background of *Wuthering Heights.*" *BST,* 13(1957):111-30.

385 MATHISON, John K. "Nelly Dean and the Power of *Wuthering Heights.*" *NCF,* 11 (1956):106-29.

386 MC KIBBEN, Robert C. "The Image of the Book in *Wuthering Heights.*" *NCF,* 15(1960):159-69.

387 MOSER, Thomas C. "What is the Matter with Emily Jane? Conflicting Impulses in *Wuthering Heights.*" *NCF,* 17(1962):1-19.*

388 [SANGER, C. P.]. *The Structure of* Wuthering Heights. London: Woolf, 1926. (Pub. as by CPS in "Hogarth Essays" series.)

389 SCHORER, Mark. "Fiction and the 'Matrix of Analogy.' " *KR,* Autumn, 1949. (Also in *Critiques and Essays on Modern Fiction, 1920-1951.* Ed. J. W. Aldridge. New York: Ronald, 1952; Brontë section in 348, pp. 356-61.)*

390 SHANNON, Edgar F., Jr. "Lockwood's Dreams and the Exegesis of *Wuthering Heights.*" *NCF,* 14(1959):95-109.

391 THOMPSON, Wade. "Infanticide and Sadism in *Wuthering Heights.*" *PMLA,* 78(1963):69-74.

392 TRAVERSI, Derek. "*Wuthering Heights* after a Hundred Years." *DubR,* 445(1949):154-68.

393 VISICK, Mary. *The Genesis of* Wuthering Heights. New York: Oxford U P, 1958.*

394 WATSON, Melvin R. "Tempest in the Soul: The Theme and Structure of *Wuthering Heights.*" *NCF,* 4(1949):87-100.

395 WATSON, Melvin R. "*Wuthering Heights* and the Critics." *Trollopian,* 3(1949):243-63. (See 18.)

396 WILLIS, Irene Cooper. *The Authorship of* Wuthering Heights. London: Hogarth, 1936. (Refutes view that Branwell had a share in it.)

397 WOODRING, Carl. "The Narrators of *Wuthering Heights.*" *NCF,* 11(1958):298-305.

398 WORTH, George J. "Emily Brontë's Mr. Lockwood." *NCF,* 12(1958):315-20.

Broughton, Rhoda (1840-1920)

MAIN NOVELS

399 *Not Wisely, but Too Well.* 3 vols., 1867. *Cometh Up as a Flower.* 2 vols., 1867. *Red as a Rose Is She.* 3 vols., 1870. *Belinda.* 3 vols., 1883. *A Fool in Her Folly*, 1920.

See 57, 89, 1754.

Bulwer-Lytton, Edward Robert [Later Lord Lytton] (1803-1873)

NOVELS

400 *Falkland.* London: Colburn, 1827. *Pelham or the Adventures of a Gentleman.* 3 vols. London: Colburn, 1828. *The Disowned.* 4 vols. London: Colburn, 1828. *Devereux.* 3 vols. London: Colburn, 1829. *Paul Clifford.* 3 vols. London: Colburn & Bentley, 1830. *Eugene Aram.* 3 vols. London: Colburn & Bentley, 1832. *Godolphin.* 3 vols. London: Colburn & Bentley, 1833. *The Last Days of Pompeii.* 3 vols. London: Bentley, 1834. *Rienzi, the Last of the Roman Tribunes.* 3 vols. London: Saunders & Otley, 1835. *Ernest Maltravers.* 3 vols. London: Saunders & Otley, 1837. *Alice, or the Mysteries.* 3 vols. London: Saunders & Otley, 1838. *Night and Morning.* 3 vols. London: Saunders & Otley, 1841. *Zanoni.* 3 vols. London: Saunders & Otley, 1842. *The Last of the Barons.* 3 vols. London: Saunders & Otley, 1843. *Lucretia, or The Children of the Night.* 3 vols. London: Saunders & Otley, 1846. *Harold, the Last of the Saxons.* 3 vols. London: Bentley, 1848. *The Caxtons, a Family Picture.* [*Blackwood's* 1848-1849.] 3 vols. Edinburgh and London: Blackwood, 1849. "*My Novel,*" by Pisistratus Caxton, or Varieties in English Life. [*Blackwood's* 1850.] 4 vols. Edinburgh and London: Blackwood, 1853. *What Will He Do with It?* by Pisistratus Caxton. [*Blackwood's* 1857.] 4 vols. Edinburgh and London: Blackwood, 1859. *A Strange Story.* [*Blackwood's* 1861.] 2 vols. Edinburgh and London: Blackwood, 1862. *The Coming Race.* [*Blackwood's* 1871.] Edinburgh and London: Blackwood, 1871. *The Parisians.* [*Blackwood's* 1872]. 4 vols. Edinburgh and London: Blackwood, 1873. *Kenelm Chillingly.* 3 vols. Edinburgh and London: Blackwood, 1873. *Pausanias the Spartan.* London: Routledge, 1876. (Unfinished historical romance.)

BIBLIOGRAPHY

See 23,* 25.*

COLLECTED EDITIONS, LETTERS

401 *The Knebworth Edition.* 37 vols. London: Routledge, 1873-1877. (Most satisfactory representation of Bulwer's poetry and nonfiction.)

402 *The New Knebworth Edition.* 29 vols. London: Routledge, 1895-1898.

403 DEVEY, Louisa, ed. *The Letters of the Late Edward Bulwer, Lord Lytton, to His Wife.* New York: Dillingham, 1889.

404 LYTTON, Edward Robert Bulwer-Lytton, First Earl of Lytton. *The Life, Letters and Literary Remains of Edward Bulwer, Lord Lytton, by His Son*. New York: Harper, 1883.

BIOGRAPHICAL AND GENERAL

405 *Bulwer and Macready: A Chronicle of the Early Victorian Theatre.* Ed. C. H. Shattuck. Urbana: U of Illinois P, 1958.

406 ESCOTT, T. H. S. *Edward Bulwer, First Baron Lytton of Knebworth. A Social, Personal, and Political Monograph.* London: Routledge, 1910.

407 LYTTON, Victor A. G. R., Second Earl. *Bulwer-Lytton*. London: Home & Van Thal, 1948.

408 LYTTON, Victor A. G. R., Second Earl. *The Life of Edward Bulwer, First Lord Lytton*. 2 vols. London: Macmillan, 1913.

409 SADLEIR, Michael. *Bulwer: A Panorama. I. Edward and Rosina, 1803-1836.* London: Constable, 1931. Repub. as *Bulwer and His Wife: A Panorama* (1933).

410 SADLEIR, Michael. *The Strange Life of Lady Blessington*. Boston: Little, Brown, 1933.

CRITICAL

See 124, 170,* 183, 185, 204.*

411 BANGS, Archie. "*Mephistophiles in England; or The Confessions of a Prime Minister.*" *PMLA* , 47(1932):200-19.

412 BELL, E. G. *Introduction to the Prose Romances, Plays and Comedies of Edward Bulwer, Lord Lytton.* Chicago: Hill, 1914.

413 DAHL, Curtis. "Bulwer-Lytton and the School of Catastrophe." *PQ*, 32(1953):428-42.

414 DAHL, Curtis. "History on the Hustings: Bulwer-Lytton's Historical Novels of Politics." In 88, pp. 60-71.*

415 FAIRCLOUGH, G. Thomas. "Bulwer-Lytton and Macaulay: A Literary Parallel." *NM*, 68(1962):68-73.

416 FRADIN, Joseph I. " 'The Absorbing Tyranny of Every-day Life': Bulwer's *A Strange Story.*" *NCF*, 16(1961):1-16.

417 LILJEGREN, S. B. *Bulwer-Lytton's Novels and Isis Unveiled.* Uppsala: Lundequistska Bokhandeln; Cambridge, Mass.: Harvard U P, 1957. (The occult element in Bulwer's novels.)

418 LLOYD, Michael. "Bulwer-Lytton and the Idealising Principle." *EM*, 7(1956):25-39.

419 MAC CARTHY, Desmond. "The Padded Man." *Experience*. London: Putnam, 1935.

420 MESSAC, Régis. "Bulwer-Lytton et Dostoïevski: de Paul Clifford à Raskolnikof." *RLC*, 6(1926):638-53.

421 ROSENBERG, Edgar. "The Jew as Parasite: Trollope and Bulwer." In 205, pp. 138-160.

422 SEIFERT, Helmut. *Bulwers Verhältnis zur Geschichte.* Munich, 1935.

423 SENIOR, Nassau. "Sir E. Bulwer-Lytton." See 92, pp. 235-320.

424 SHEPPARD, Alred Tresidder. *The Art and Practice of Historical Fiction.* London: Toulmin, 1930.

425 STEVENSON, Lionel. "Stepfathers of Victorianism." *VQR,* 6(1930):251-67.

426 WAGNER, Geoffrey. "A Forgotten Satire: Bulwer-Lytton's *The Coming Race.*" *NCF,* 19(1965):379-85.

427 WATTS, Harold H. "Lytton's Theories of Prose and Fiction." *PMLA,* 50(1935):274-89.

Butler, Samuel (1835-1902)

NOVELS

428 *Erewhon, or Over the Range.* London: Trubner, 1872. *Erewhon Revisted Twenty Years Later Both by the Original Discoverer of the Country and by His Son.* London: Richards, 1901. *The Way of All Flesh.* London: Richards, 1903. (Published posthumously.)

BIBLIOGRAPHY

429 *English Literature in Transition (ELT).* (Contains annual bibliographies of work on Samuel Butler.)

430 HARKNESS, S. B. *The Career of Samuel Butler: A Bibliography.* London: Bodley Head, 1955.

431 HOLT, Lee E. "Samuel Butler's Revisions of *Erewhon.*" *PBSA,* 38(1944):22-38.

COLLECTIONS

432 COLE, G. D. H., ed. *The Essential Samuel Butler.* New York: Dutton, 1950.

NOTEBOOKS AND LETTERS

433 JONES, Henry Festing, and A. T. BARTHOLOMEW, eds. *Works.* The Shrewsbury Edition. 20 vols. New York: Dutton, 1923-1926.

434 BARTHOLOMEW, A. T., ed. *Butleriana.* London: Nonesuch, 1932. (Unpub. portions of the Notebooks.)

435 BARTHOLOMEW, A. T., ed. *Further Extracts from the Notebooks of Samuel Butler.* London: Cape, 1934.

436 HOWARD, Daniel F., ed. *The Correspondence of Samuel Butler with His Sister May.* Berkeley: U of California P, 1962.

437 KEYNES, Geoffrey, and Brian HILL. *Butler's Notebooks: Selections.* New York: Dutton, 1951.

438 *Letters between Samuel Butler and Miss E. M. Savage, 1871-1885.* London: Cape, 1935.

439 SILVER, Arnold, ed. *The Family Letters of Samuel Butler, 1841-1886.* Stanford: Stanford U P, 1962.

BIOGRAPHICAL AND GENERAL

440 BISSELL, Claude. "The Butlerian Inheritance of G. B. Shaw." *DR*, 41(1961):159-73.

441 FURBANK, P. N. *Samuel Butler (1835-1902).* Cambridge, Eng.: Cambridge U P, 1948.*

442 HENDERSON, Philip. *Samuel Butler: The Incarnate Bachelor.* London: Cohen & West, 1953.*

443 HOLT, Lee E. *Samuel Butler.* New York: Twayne, 1964.

444 JONES, Henry Festing. *Samuel Butler, Author of* Erewhon *(1835-1902): A Memoir.* 2 vols. London: Macmillan, 1919.*

445 MUGGERIDGE, Malcolm. *The Earnest Atheist: A Study of Samuel Butler.* London: Putnam, 1936.

446 STILLMAN, Clara G. *Samuel Butler, a Mid-Victorian Modern.* New York: Viking, 1932.

447 WILLEY, Basil. *Darwin and Butler: Two Versions of Evolution.* London: Chatto & Windus; New York: Harcourt, Brace, 1960.

CRITICISM

448 O'CONNOR, William Van. "Samuel Butler and Bloomsbury." In 88, pp. 257-73.*

449 ZABEL, Morton Dauwen. "Samuel Butler: The Victorian Insolvency." *Craft and Character in Modern Fiction.* New York: Viking, 1957, pp. 97-113.*

Erewhon

450 DYSON, A. E. "Samuel Butler: The Honest Sceptic." *The Crazy Fabric: Essays in Irony.* London and New York: Macmillan, 1965, pp. 114-37. (Mainly on *Erewhon*, though also on *Erewhon Revisited* and *The Way of All Flesh.*)*

451 FORSTER, E. M. "A Book That Influenced Me." *Two Cheers for Democracy.* New York: Harcourt, Brace, 1951, pp. 224-8.

452 LEYBURN, Ellen Douglass. *Satiric Allegory: Mirror for Man.* New Haven: Yale U P, 1956, pp. 92-106.

The Way of All Flesh

453 BISSELL, Claude. "A Study of *The Way of All Flesh.*" *Nineteenth-Century Studies.* Eds. Herbert Davis, William C. DeVane, and R. C. Bald. Ithaca: Cornell U P, 1940, pp. 277-303.

454 COLE, G. D. H. *Samuel Butler and* The Way of All Flesh. London: Home & Van Thal, 1947.

455 HOWARD, Daniel F. "The Critical Significance of Autobiography in *The Way of All Flesh*." *VN*, 17(1960):1-3.

456 HOWARD, Daniel F., ed. *Ernest Pontifex, or The Way of All Flesh*. Boston: Houghton Mifflin, 1964. (Annotated, with an introduction by the editor.)*†

457 KETTLE, Arnold. "Samuel Butler: *The Way of All Flesh*." In 71, Vol. II, pp. 35-48.*

458 KNOEPFLMACHER, U. C. " 'Ishmael' or Anti-Hero? The Division of Self: *The Way of All Flesh*." *EFT* [now *ELT*], 4(1961):28-35.

459 KNOEPFLMACHER, U. C. "Reality and Utopia in *The Way of All Flesh*." In 187, pp. 257-95.*

460 LIND, Ilse Dusoir. "*The Way of All Flesh* and *A Portrait of the Artist as a Young Man:* A Comparison." *VN*, 9(1956):7-10.

461 MARSHALL, William H. "The Use of Symbols in *The Way of All Flesh*." *TSLL*, 10(1965):109-21. See 77, pp. 425-449.

462 SHAW, George Bernard. "Samuel Butler." Introduction to *The Way of All Flesh*. WC. London: Oxford U P, 1936.

463 SHOENBERG, Robert E. "The Literal-Mindedness of Samuel Butler." *SEL*, 4(1964):601-16.

Carleton, William (1794–1869)

MAIN NOVELS

464 *Fardorougha the Miser; or, the Convicts of Lisnamona*, 1839. *Valentine McClutchy, the Irish Agent; or, Chronicles of the Castle Cumber Property.* 3 vols. 1845. *The Black Prophet: A Tale of Irish Famine*, 1847. *The Emigrants of Ahadarra; A Tale of Irish Life*, 1848. *The Tithe-Proctor*, 1849. *Willy Reilly and His Dear Cooleen Bawn: A Tale Founded upon Fact.* 3 vols., 1855.

STUDIES

465 FLANAGAN, Thomas B. "William Carleton." In 38, pp. 255-330.

466 KIELY, Benedict. *Poor Scholar: A Study of the Works and Days of William Carleton*. New York: Sheed & Ward, 1948.

"Carroll, Lewis" (Dodgson, Charles Lutwidge) (1832–1898)

NOVELS

467 *Alice's Adventures in Wonderland*. London: Macmillan, 1865. *Through the Looking-Glass, and What Alice Found There*. London: Macmillan, 1872. *Sylvie and Bruno*. London: Macmillan, 1889. *Sylvie and Bruno Concluded*. London: Macmillan, 1893.

COLLECTED EDITIONS, DIARIES, LETTERS

468 *The Complete Works of Lewis Carroll.* Introduction by Alexander Woolcott. Illustrations by Tenniel. New York: Modern Library, 1936.

469 GREEN, Roger Lancelyn, ed. *The Diaries of Lewis Carroll.* 2 vols. New York: Oxford U P, 1954.

470 HATCH, Evelyn M., ed. *A Selection from the Letters of Lewis Carroll to His Child-Friends.* London: Macmillan, 1933.

471 WILLIAMS, S. H., and F. MADAN. *The Lewis Carroll Handbook* [1931]. Rev. R. L. Green. New York: Oxford U P, 1962.

BIOGRAPHICAL AND CRITICAL

472 COLLINGWOOD, Stuart Dodgson. *The Life and Letters of Lewis Carroll.* London: Unwin, 1898. (Repr. Detroit: Gale, 1968.)

473 DE LA MARE, Walter. *Lewis Carroll.* London: Faber, 1932.

474 GREEN, Roger Lancelyn. *The Story of Lewis Carroll.* New York: Schumann, 1949.

475 GREENACRE, Phyllis. *Swift and Carroll; a Psychoanalytic Study of Two Lives.* New York: International U P, 1955.

476 HUDSON, Derek. *Lewis Carroll.* London: Longmans, 1958.

477 LENNON, Florence B. *The Life of Lewis Carroll.* New York: Crowell-Collier, 1962. [A rev. ed. of her *Victoria through the Looking-Glass.* New York: Simon & Schuster, 1945.]†

478 PITCHER, George. "Wittgenstein, Nonsense and Lewis Carroll." *MR,* 6(1965):591–611.

479 SEWELL, Elizabeth. *Field of Nonsense.* London: Chatto & Windus, 1952.

480 TAYLOR, A. L. *The White Knight: A Study of C. L. Dodgson (Lewis Carroll).* Edinburgh: Oliver & Boyd, 1952.*

481 WILSON, Edmund. "C. L. Dodgson: The Poet Logician." *The Shores of Light.* New York: Farrar, Straus & Young, 1952, pp. 540–50.†

482 WOOLF, Virginia. "Lewis Carroll." *The Moment and Other Essays.* London: Hogarth, 1947, pp. 70–71.

ALICE IN WONDERLAND AND THROUGH THE LOOKING GLASS

483 GARDNER, Martin. *The Annotated Alice.* New York: Potter, 1960. (Includes *Alice's Adventures in Wonderland, Through the Looking Glass,* and a selected bibliography.)*†

484 RACKIN, Donald, ed. *Alice's Adventures in Wonderland: A Critical Handbook.* Belmont, Calif.: Wadsworth, 1969.*

485 AYRES, H. M. *Carroll's Alice.* New York: Columbia U P, 1936.

486 BOYNTON, Mary Fuertes. "An Oxford Don Quixote." *Hispania,* 47(1964):738–50. (Compares *Alice* books and *Don Quixote.*)

487 EMPSON, William. "Alice in Wonderland: The Child as Swain." *Some Versions of Pastoral.* New York: New Directions, 1938, pp. 253-94.*†

488 LEVIN, Harry. "Wonderland Revisited." *KR,* 27(1965):591-616.*

489 RACKIN, Donald. "Alice's Journey to the End of the Night." *PMLA,* 81(1966):313-26.

490 RACKIN, Donald. "Corrective Laughter: Carroll's Alice and Popular Children's Literature of the Nineteenth Century." *JPC,* 1(1967):192-201.

Cobbold, Richard (1797-1877)

MAIN NOVEL

491 *The History of Margaret Catchpole, a Suffolk Girl.* 3 vols., 1845.

Collins, (William) Wilkie (1824-1889)

NOVELS

492 *Antonina: or the Fall of Rome. A Romance of the Fifth Century.* 3 vols. London: Bentley, 1850. *Basil: A Story of Modern Life.* 3 vols. London: Bentley, 1852. *Hide and Seek.* 3 vols. London: Bentley, 1854. *The Dead Secret.* [*Household Words,* 1857.] 2 vols. London: Bradbury & Evans, 1857. *The Woman in White.* [*All the Year Round,* 1859-1860.] 3 vols. London: Low, 1860. *No Name.* [*All the Year Round,* 1862-1863.] 3 vols. London: Low, 1862. *Armadale.* [*Cornhill Mag.* and *Harpers Mag.,* 1864-1865.] 2 vols. London: Smith, Elder, 1866. *The Moonstone: A Romance.* [*All the Year Round,* 1868]. 3 vols. London: Tinsley, 1868. *Man and Wife.* 3 vols. London: Ellis, 1870. *Poor Miss Finch.* [*Cassell's Mag.,* 1871.] 3 vols. London: Bentley, 1872. *The New Magdalen.* [*Temple Bar Mag.,* 1872.] 2 vols. London: Bentley, 1873. *The Law and the Lady: A Novel.* 3 vols. London: Chatto & Windus, 1875. *The Two Destinies: A Romance.* 2 vols. London: Chatto & Windus, 1876. *The Haunted Hotel: A Mystery of Modern Venice.* [*Belgravia,* 1875.] 2 vols. London: Chatto & Windus, 1879. *A Rogue's Life: From His Birth to His Marriage.* [*Household Words,* 1856.] London: Bentley, 1879. *The Fallen Leaves.* First Series. 3 vols. London: Chatto & Windus, 1879. (Not continued.) *Jezebel's Daughter.* 3 vols. London: Chatto & Windus, 1880. *The Black Robe.* [*Canadian Monthly.*] 3 vols. London: Chatto & Windus, 1881. *Heart and Science. A Story of the Present Time.* [*Belgravia,* 1882.] 3 vols. London: Chatto & Windus, 1883. *I Say No.* 3 vols. London: Chatto & Windus, 1884. *The Evil Genius: A Domestic Story.* 3 vols. London: Chatto & Windus, 1886. *The Legacy of Cain.* 3 vols. London: Chatto & Windus, 1889. *Blind Love.* [*Illustrated London Magazine,* 1889. First eighteen weekly parts by Collins; completed by Walter Besant from Collins's synopsis.] 3 vols. London: Chatto & Windus, 1890.

BIBLIOGRAPHY

See 25.*

493 ANDREW, A. V. "A Wilkie Collins Check-List." *ESA,* 3(1960):79-98.

494 ASHLEY, Robert P. "The Wilkie Collins Collection." *PULC*, 17(1956):81-4.

495 CORDASCO, Francesco, and Kenneth SCOTT. *Wilkie Collins and Charles Reade: A Bibliography of Critical Notices and Studies.* Brooklyn: Long Island U P, 1949.

496 PARRISH, M. L. *Wilkie Collins and Charles Reade.* London: Constable, 1940. (Listing and description of first eds.)

COLLECTED EDITIONS

There is no complete or reliable collected edition.

497 *The Works of Wilkie Collins.* 30 vols. New York: Collier, ca. 1900.

498 *Novels.* Library Edition. 18 vols. London: Chatto & Windus, 1905-1909.

BIOGRAPHICAL

499 ASHLEY, Robert. *Wilkie Collins.* London: Barker, 1952.

500 DAVIS, Nuel P. *The Life of Wilkie Collins.* Introduction by Gordon N. Ray. Urbana: U of Illinois P, 1956.

501 ROBINSON, Kenneth. *Wilkie Collins: A Biography.* London: Bodley Head, 1951.*

CRITICAL

See 62, 177, 203.

502 ASHLEY, Robert. "Wilkie Collins and the Detective Story." *NCF*, 6(1951):47-60.

503 ASHLEY, Robert. "Wilkie Collins Reconsidered." *NCF*, 4(1950):265-73.

504 BOOTH, Bradford. "Wilkie Collins and the Art of Fiction." *NCF*, 6(1951):131-45.*

505 BURGESS, Anthony. Introduction to *The Moonstone*. With notes by David Williams. London: Pan, 1967.†

506 CORRIGAN, Beatrice. "Antonio Fogazzaro and Wilkie Collins." *CL*, 13(1961):39-51.

507 DE LA MARE, Walter. "The Early Novels of Wilkie Collins." See 37.

508 ELIOT, T. S. "Wilkie Collins and Dickens." *Selected Essays.* Rev. ed. New York: Harcourt, Brace, 1950.

509 HYDER, Clyde K. "Wilkie Collins and *The Woman in White*." *PMLA*, 54(1939):297-303.*

510 LAWSON, Lewis A. "Wilkie Collins and the *Moonstone*." *AI.*, 20(1963):61-79.

511 MC CLEARY, G. F. "A Victorian Classic." *FR*, 160(1946):137-41. (*The Moonstone.*)

512 MAC EACHEN, Dougald. "Wilkie Collins and British Law." *NCF* 5(1950):121-39.

513 MILLEY, H. J. W. *"The Eustace Diamonds* and *The Moonstone." SP*, 36(1939):651–63.

514 MILLEY, H. J. W. "Wilkie Collins and *A Tale of Two Cities." MLR*, 34(1939):525–34.

515 RYCROFT, Charles. *Imagination and Reality: Psycho-Analytical Essays 1951–1961.* International Psychoanalytic Library 75. Introduction by M. Masud, R. Khan, and John D. Sutherland. London: Hogarth, 1968. (Essay on *The Moonstone.*)

516 STEWART, J. I. M., ed. *The Moonstone.* London: Penguin, 1966.†

517 SWINBURNE, Algernon C. *Studies in Prose and Poetry.* London, 1894.

518 TILLOTSON, Geoffrey. "Wilkie Collins' *No Name.*" In 96, pp. 231–43.*

519 TILLOTSON, Kathleen. Introduction to *The Woman in White.* Ed. Anthea White. Boston: Houghton Mifflin, 1969.†

520 WOLFE, Peter. "Point of View and Characterization in Wilkie Collins' *The Moonstone." ForumH*, 4(1965):27–9.

Craik, Mrs.

See below under MULOCK.

Dickens, Charles (1812–1870)

NOVELS

521 *The Posthumous Papers of the Pickwick Club.* [20 as 19 nos., 1836–1837.] London: Chapman & Hall, 1837. *Oliver Twist, or, The Parish Boy's Progress. By "Boz."* [*Bentley's Misc.,* Feb. 1837–April 1839.] 3 vols. London: Bentley, 1838. *The Life and Adventures of Nicholas Nickleby.* [20 as 19 nos., 1838–1839.] London: Chapman & Hall, 1839. *The Old Curiosity Shop.* [As first part of *Master Humphrey's Clock.* 88 weekly nos., 20 monthly nos., 1840–1841.] London: Chapman & Hall, 1841. *Barnaby Rudge.* [As second part of *Master Humphrey's Clock.* 88 weekly nos., 20 monthly nos., 1840–1841.] London: Chapman & Hall, 1841. *The Life and Adventures of Martin Chuzzlewit.* [20 as 19 nos., 1843–1844.] London: Chapman & Hall, 1844. *Dealings with the Firm of Dombey and Son Wholesale, Retail, and for Exportation.* [20 as 19 nos., 1846–1848.] London: Bradbury & Evans, 1848. *The Personal History, Adventures, Experiences, and Observations of David Copperfield the Younger.* [20 as 19 nos., 1849–1850.] London: Bradbury & Evans, 1850. *Bleak House.* [20 as 19 nos., 1852–1853.] London: Bradbury & Evans, 1853. *Hard Times for These Times.* [*Household Words,* April-Aug. 1854.] London: Bradbury & Evans, 1854. *Little Dorrit.* [20 as 19 nos., 1855–1857.] London: Bradbury & Evans, 1857.

522 *A Tale of Two Cities.* [In *All the Year Round,* April–Nov., and in 8 as 7 nos., June–Dec. 1859.] London: Chapman & Hall, 1859. *Great Expectations.* [*All the Year Round,* Dec. 1860–Aug. 1861.] 3 vols. London: Chapman & Hall, 1861. *Our Mutual Friend.* [20 as 19 nos., 1864–1865.] 2 vols. London: Chapman & Hall, 1865. *The Mystery of Edwin Drood.* [Monthly nos. from April 1870; ended at 6th no. by Dickens's death.] London: Chapman & Hall, 1870.

BIBLIOGRAPHY AND REFERENCE

See 25, 590.

523 *Dickensian, The.* 1905– . (In progress. Index for 1905–1934, 1953; for 1935–1960, 1961. Contains lists and reviews of current Dickensiana.)

524 ECKEL, John C. *The First Editions of the Writings of Charles Dickens.* London: Chapman & Hall, 1913. Rev. and enl. New York: Inman; London: Maggs, 1932.

525 FIELDING, K. J. *Charles Dickens.* WTW. London and New York: Longmans, Green, 1953. Rev. 1960, 1963. (A bibliographical survey of criticism.)†

526 FORD, George H., and Lauriat LANE, Jr., eds. *The Dickens Critics.* Ithaca: Cornell U P, 1961. (Repr. of notable Dickens criticism from Poe to Trilling: bibliography, indices, checklist of criticism 1840–1960.)*†

527 HATTON, Thomas, and Arthur H. CLEAVER. *A Bibliography of the Periodical Works of Charles Dickens.* London: Chapman & Hall, 1933.

528 HAYWARD, Arthur L. *The Dickens Encyclopedia: An Alphabetical Dictionary of References to Every Character and Place Mentioned in the Works of Fiction.* Hamden, Conn.: Archon, 1968.

529 MILLER, William. *The Dickens Student and Collector: A List of Writings Relating to Charles Dickens and His Works, 1836–1945.* Cambridge, Mass.: Harvard U P, 1946. (Supps., Brighton, 1947; Hove, 1963.)

530 PIERCE, Gilbert A. *The Dickens Dictionary.* London, 1872; 2d ed. with additions by W. A. Wheeler, 1894. Rev. ed. Boston and New York: Houghton, Mifflin, 1965.

TEXTS: COLLECTED EDITIONS AND LETTERS

531 *The Works of Charles Dickens.* 21 vols. London: Chapman & Hall, 1867–1875. (The Charles Dickens Edition.)

532 *The Works of Charles Dickens.* Introduction by Charles Dickens the Younger. 21 vols. London: Macmillan, 1892–1925.

533 *The Works of Charles Dickens.* Introduction, general essay, and notes by Andrew Lang. 36 vols. London: Chapman & Hall; New York: Scribner's, 1897–1908. (Gadshill Edition.)*

534 *The Nonesuch Dickens.* 23 vols. Bloomsbury: Nonesuch, 1937–1938. (Limited and expensive edition.)*

535 *Oxford Illustrated Dickens.* 21 vols. Oxford: Oxford U P, 1947–1958.*

536 *The Clarendon Dickens*. Eds. John Butt and Kathleen Tillotson. London and New York: Oxford U P, 1966- . (The first ed. to be based on full collation of texts. Only *Oliver Twist* pub. by 1967.)*

LETTERS

537 DEXTER, Walter, ed. *Letters of Charles Dickens*. 3 vols. London: Constable, 1938. (Nonesuch Edition; fullest collection—5,811 letters.)*

538 DEXTER, Walter, ed. *Mr. and Mrs. Charles Dickens: His Letters to Her.* London: Constable, 1935.

539 DUPEE, F. W., ed. *The Selected Letters of Charles Dickens*. Great Letters Series. New York: Farrar, Straus & Cudahy, 1960.

540 HOUSE, Madeline, and Graham STOREY, eds. *The Letters of Charles Dickens*. Vol. I: 1820-1839; Vol II: 1840-1841. Oxford: Clarendon P, 1965, 1969. (Pilgrim Edition—projected definitive ed. in 12 volumes of over 12,000 letters.)*

541 JOHNSON, Edgar. *The Heart of Charles Dickens*. Boston: Little, Brown, 1952; issued in England as *Letters from Charles Dickens to Angela Burdett-Coutts*. London: Cape, 1953.

BIOGRAPHICAL AND GENERAL STUDIES

542 ADRIAN, Arthur A. *Georgina Hogarth and the Dickens Circle*. London and New York: Oxford U P, 1957.

543 BROWN, Ivor. *Dickens in His Time*. London: Nelson, 1963.

544 CRUIKSHANK, R. J. *Charles Dickens and Early Victorian England.* London: Pitman, 1949.

545 FORSTER, John. *The Life of Charles Dickens* [3 vols. 1872-1874]. Ed. and annotated by J. W. T. Ley. New York: Doubleday, Doran, 1928.*

546 HEILMAN, Robert B. "The New World in Dickens's Writings." 2 parts; *Trollopian* [see 18], 3(1946):25-43; 4(1947):11-26.

547 HIBBERT, Christopher. *The Making of Charles Dickens*. London: Longmans, Green, 1967.

548 JACKSON, Thomas A. *Charles Dickens: The Progress of a Radical*. London: Lawrence & Wishart, 1937. (Marxist approach.)*

549 JOHNSON, Edgar. *Charles Dickens: His Tragedy and Triumph*. 2 vols. New York: Simon & Schuster, 1952.*

550 LEY, J. W. T. *The Dickens Circle: A Narrative of the Novelist's Friendships.* London: Chapman & Hall, 1918.

551 LINDSAY, Jack. *Charles Dickens: A Biographical and Critical Study*. New York: Philosophical Library, 1950.

552 NISBET, Ada. *Dickens and Ellen Ternan*. Foreword by Edmund Wilson. Berkeley and Los Angeles: U of California P, 1952.*

553 PEARSON, Hesketh. *Charles Dickens: His Character, Comedy, and Career.* New York: Harper, 1949.

554 POPE-HENNESSY, Una. *Charles Dickens*. New York: Howell, Soskin, 1945.

555 PRIESTLEY, J. B. *Charles Dickens: A Pictorial Biography*. London: Thames & Hudson, 1961; New York: Viking, 1962.

556 STOREY, Gladys. *Dickens and Daughter*. London: Muller, 1939.

557 SYMONS, Julian. *Charles Dickens*. London: Barker, 1951.

558 WAGENKNECHT, Edward. *The Man Charles Dickens: A Victorian Portrait*. Boston and New York: Houghton Mifflin, 1929. Rev. ed. Norman: U of Oklahoma P, 1966.

SURVEYS AND COLLECTIONS OF CRITICISM

See 526.*

559 CLARK, William R., ed. *Discussions of Dickens*. Boston: Heath, 1961.†

560 FORD, George H. *Dickens and His Readers: Aspects of Novel-Criticism since 1836*. Princeton: Princeton U P, 1955.†

561 GROSS, John, and Gabriel PEARSON, eds. *Dickens and the Twentieth Century*. London: Routledge & Kegan Paul; Toronto: U of Toronto P, 1962. (Collection of essays commissioned for 150th anniversary of Dickens's birth.)*†

562 PEYROUTON, Noel, ed. *Dickens Criticism: A Symposium*. Cambridge, Mass.: Dickens Reference Center, 1962.

563 PRICE, Martin, ed. *Dickens: A Collection of Critical Essays*. TCV. Englewood Cliffs, N.J.: Prentice-Hall, 1967.†

564 RANTAVAARA, Irma. *Dickens in the Light of English Criticism*. Helsingfors: Akademisk, 1944.

CRITICAL AND OTHER STUDIES

See 52,* 200, 201.

565 AXTON, W. F. *Circle of Fire: Dickens's Vision and Style and the Popular Victorian Theatre*. Lexington: U of Kentucky P, 1966.

566 BLOUNT, Trevor. *Dickens: The Early Novels*. WTW. London: Longmans, Green, 1968.

567 BODELSON, C. A. "The Physiognomy of the Name." *REL*, 2, iii(1961):39-48. Repr. in *Essays and Papers Presented to C. A. Bodelson*. Copenhagen, 1964.

568 BODELSON, C. A. "Some Notes on Dickens' Symbolism." *ES*, 40(1959):420-31. Also repr. in 567.

569 BOEGE, Fred W. "Point of View in Dickens." *PMLA*, 65(1950):90-105.

570 BUSH, Douglas. "A Note on Dickens' Humor." In 88, pp. 82-91, and in his *Engaged and Disengaged*. Cambridge, Mass.: Harvard U P, 1966.

571 BUTT, John, and Kathleen TILLOTSON. *Dickens at Work*. London: Methuen, 1957; New York: Oxford U P, 1958. (Study of methods of composition and revision.)*

572 CHESTERTON, G. K. *Appreciations and Criticisms of the Works of Charles Dickens*. London: Dent, 1911. (Reissued as *Criticisms and Appreciations*, 1933. Collection of his introductions to the Everyman Edition.)*

573 CHESTERTON, G. K. *Charles Dickens: A Critical Study*. New York: Dodd, Mead, 1906. Repr. with introduction by Alexander Woolcott, as *Charles Dickens: The Last of the Great Men*, 1942. With introduction by Steven Marcus.†

574 CHRISTIAN, Mildred G. "Carlyle's Influence upon the Social Theory of Dickens." *Trollopian* [see 18], 4(1947):27-35.

575 CHURCHILL, R. C. "Dickens, Drama, and Tradition." *Scrutiny*, 10(1942):358-75.

576 COCKSHUT, A. O. J. *The Imagination of Charles Dickens*. London: Collins, 1961; New York: New York U P, 1962.

577 COLLINS, Philip. *Dickens and Crime*. London: Macmillan; New York: St Martin's P, 1962.*

578 COLLINS, Philip. *Dickens and Education*. London: Macmillan; New York: St Martin's P, 1963.*

579 COLLINS, Philip. "Dickens and *Punch*." *DiS*, 3(1967):4-21.

580 COLLINS, Philip. "Queen Mab's Chariot among the Steam Engines: Dickens and Fancy." *ES*, 42(1961):78-90.

581 COOLIDGE, Archibald C., Jr. *Dickens as a Serial Novelist*. Ames: Iowa State U P, 1967.

582 COOPERMAN, Stanley. "Dickens and the Secular Blasphemy: Social Criticism in *Hard Times*, *Little Dorrit*, and *Bleak House*." *CE*, 22(1960):156-60.

583 COVENEY, Peter. "The Child in Dickens." In 172.

584 COX, C. B. "In Defense of Dickens." *E&S*, 11(1958):86-100.

585 DABNEY, Ross H. *Love and Property in the Novels of Dickens*. Berkeley: U of California P; London: Chatto & Windus, 1967.

586 DAVIS, Earle. *The Flint and the Flame: The Artistry of Charles Dickens*. Columbia: U of Missouri P, 1963.

587 DIBELIUS, Wilhelm. *Charles Dickens*. Leipzig: Teubner, 1926.

588 DONOVAN, Frank R. *Dickens and Youth*. New York: Dodd Mead, 1968.

589 DUPEE, F. W. "The Other Dickens." *"The King of the Cats"* and Other Remarks on Writers and Writings. New York: Noonday P, 1965.†

590 EISENSTEIN, Sergei. "Dickens, Griffith, and the Film Today." *Film Form*. Newly trans. and ed. by Jay Leyda. New York: Meridian, 1960.†

591 ELIOT, T. S. "Wilkie Collins and Dickens." See 508.

592 ENGEL, Monroe. *The Maturity of Dickens*. Cambridge, Mass.: Harvard U P, 1959.

593 FANGER, Donald. *Dostoevsky and Romantic Realism*. Cambridge, Mass.: Harvard U P, 1965.

594 FIELDING, K. J. *Charles Dickens: A Critical Introduction.* London and New York: Longmans, Green, 1958; 2d ed. rev. and enl., 1964.*†

595 FIELDING, Kenneth J. "Dickens and the Past: The Novelist of Memory." *Experience in the Novel.* Ed. Roy Harvey Pearce. Selected Papers from the English Institute. New York: Columbia U P, 1968, pp. 107-131.

596 GARIS, Robert. *The Dickens Theatre: A Reassessment of the Novels.* Oxford: Clarendon P, 1965.*

597 GERSON, Stanley. *Sound and Symbol in the Dialogue of the Works of Charles Dickens.* Stockholm Studies in English Literature 19. Stockholm: Almqvist & Wiksell, 1967.

598 GIBSON, Priscilla. "Dickens' Uses of Animism." *NCF,* 7(1953):283-91.

599 GISSING, George. *Charles Dickens: A Critical Study.* London, 1898; rev., 1903.

600 GISSING, George. *Critical Studies of the Works of Charles Dickens.* New York: Greenberg, 1924. [London title, *The Immortal Dickens,* 1925.]

601 GREENE, Graham. "The Young Dickens." *The Lost Childhood.* London: Eyre & Spottiswoode, 1951, pp. 51-57.†

602 GRUBB, Gerald G. "Dickens' Pattern of Weekly Serialization." *ELH,* 9(1942):141-56.

603 GRUBB, Gerald G. "The Editorial Policies of Charles Dickens." *PMLA,* 58(1943):1110-24.

604 HARDY, Barbara. "The Change of Heart in Dickens' Novels." *VS,* 5(1961):49-67.

605 HARDY, Barbara. *Dickens: The Later Novels.* WTW. London: Longmans, 1968.

606 HORSMAN, Ernest Allen. *Dickens and the Structure of the Novel.* Dunedin: U of Otago P, 1959.*

607 HOUSE, Humphry. *The Dickens World.* New York and London: Oxford U P, 1941.*†

608 HOUSE, Humphry. *All in Due Time.* London: Hart-Davis, 1955. (On *Great Expectations* and *Oliver Twist.*)

609 JARMUTH, Sylvia L. *Dickens' Use of Women in His Novels.* New York: Excelsior, 1967.

610 JOHNSON, Edward D. H. *Charles Dickens: An Introduction to His Novels.* New York: Random House, 1969.

611 JOHNSON, Edgar. "Dickens and Shaw: Critics of Society." *VQR,* 33(1957):66-79.

612 KARL, Frederick R. "Charles Dickens: The Victorian Quixote." In 42, pp. 105-76.

613 KELLY, Thomas. "Character in Dickens' Late Novels." *MLQ,* 30(1969):386-401.

614 KETTLE, Arnold. "Dickens and the Popular Tradition." *Carleton Miscellany,* 3(1961):17-51.

615 LANE, Lauriat, Jr. "Dickens' Archetypal Jew." *PMLA*, 73(1958):94–100.

616 MC MASTER, R. D. "Dickens and the Horrific." *DR*, 38(1958):18–20.

617 MC MASTER, R. D. "Man into Beast in Dickensian Caricature." *UTQ*, 31(1962):354–61.

618 MANHEIM, Leonard F. "Floras and Doras: The Women in Dickens' Novels." *TSLL*, 7(1965):181–200.

619 MARCUS, Steven. *Dickens: From Pickwick to Dombey.* New York: Basic Books, 1964.*

620 MILLER, J. Hillis: *Charles Dickens: The World of His Novels.* Cambridge, Mass.: Harvard U P, 1958.*

621 MONOD, Sylvère. *Dickens romancier; ètude sur la création littéraire dans les romans de Charles Dickens.* Paris: Hachette, 1953. (Trans. as *Dickens the Novelist.* Norman: U of Oklahoma P, 1967.)

622 MONOD, Sylvère. "A French View of Dickens's Humour." *REL*, 2(1961):29–38.

623 O'CONNOR, Frank. "Dickens: The Intrusion of the Audience." *The Mirror in the Roadway.* New York: Knopf, 1956, pp. 70–82.

624 ORWELL, George. "Charles Dickens" [1939]. *Dickens, Dali, and Others: Studies in Popular Culture.* New York: Reynal & Hitchcock, 1946. (Repub. in various forms including *A Collection of Essays by George Orwell.* Garden City, N.Y.: Doubleday, 1954.)*†

625 PRITCHETT, V. S. "The Humour of Dickens." *Listener,* June 3, 1954. (Rev. and repr. as "The Comic World of Dickens," in 526.)*

626 QUILLER-COUCH, Arthur. *Charles Dickens and Other Victorians.* Cambridge: Cambridge U P, 1925.

627 QUIRK, Randolph. *Dickens and Appropriate Language.* Durham, Eng.: U of Durham P, 1959.

628 QUIRK, Randolph. "Some Observations on the Language of Dickens." *REL*, 2(1961):19–28.

629 RALEIGH, John Henry. "Dickens and the Sense of Time." *NCF*, 13(1958):127–37.

630 REID, J. C. *The Hidden World of Charles Dickens.* Auckland: U of Auckland P, 1962.

631 ROOKE, Eleanor. "Fathers and Sons in Charles Dickens." *E&S*, n.s.4(1951):141–53.

632 ROSENBERG, Marvin. "The Dramatist in Dickens." *JEGP*, 59(1960):1–12.

633 SACKVILLE-WEST, Edward. "Dickens and the World of Childhood." *Inclinations.* London: Secker & Warburg, 1949.

634 SANTAYANA, George. "Dickens." *Soliloquies in England.* New York: Scribner's, 1922. Repr. in *Essays in Literary Criticism.* Ed. Irving Singer. New York: Scribner's, 1956.*†

635 SENNEWALD, Charlotte. *Die Namengebung bei Dickens, eine Studie über Lautsymbolik.* Leipzig: Mayer & Muller, 1936.

636 SIMPSON, Evelyn. "Jonson and Dickens: A Study in the Comic Genius of London." *E&S*, 29(1943):82–92.

637 SMITH, Grahame. *Dickens, Money, and Society*. Berkeley: U of California P, 1968.

638 SMITH, Sheila M. "Anti-Mechanism and the Comic in the Writings of Charles Dickens." *RMS*, 3(1959):131–44.

639 SPILKA, Mark. *Dickens and Kafka: A Mutual Interpretation*. Bloomington: Indiana U P, 1963.

640 STEVENSON, Lionel. "Dickens's Dark Novels, 1851–1857." *SR*, 51(1943):398–409.

641 STOEHR, Taylor. *Dickens: The Dreamer's Stance*. Ithaca: Cornell U P, 1965.*

642 STONE, Harry. "Dickens and Interior Monologue," *PQ*, 38(1959):52–65.

643 STONE, Harry. "Dickens and the Jews." *VS*, 2(1959):223–53.

644 TAINE, Hippolyte. *A History of English Literature*. 4 vols. [1st ed. 1851–1863.] Trans. H. van Laun. New York: J. W. Lovell, 1873. (Fine discussion of Dickens's early work, Book V, Ch. I.)†

645 WAGENKNECHT, Edward. *Dickens and the Scandalmongers: Essays in Criticism*. Norman: U of Oklahoma P, 1965.

646 WELSH, Alexander. "Satire and History: The City of Dickens." *VS*, 11(1968):379–400.

647 WILSON, Angus. "Charles Dickens: A Haunting." *CritQ*, 2(1960):101–8.*

648 WILSON, Angus. "The Heroes and Heroines of Dickens." *REL*, 2 (1961):9–18.*

649 WILSON, Edmund. *The Wound and the Bow*. New York: Oxford U P, 1947.*†

650 WINTERS, Warrington. "Dickens and the Psychology of Dreams." *PMLA*, 63(1948):984–1006.

651 YAMAMOTO, Tadao. *Growth and System of the Language of Dickens: An Introduction to a Dickens Lexicon*. Osaka: Kansai U P, 1950; rev. ed., 1952.

See individual essays in 572,* 600.

BARNABY RUDGE

652 DYSON, A. E. "*Barnaby Rudge:* The Genesis of Violence." *CritQ*, 9(1967):142–60.

653 FOLLAND, Harold F. "The Doer and the Deed: Theme and Pattern in *Barnaby Rudge*." *PMLA*, 74(1959):406–17.

654 GOTTSHALL, James K. "Devils Abroad, the Unity and Significance of *Barnaby Rudge*." *NCF*, 16(1961):133–46.

655 LINDSAY, Jack. "*Barnaby Rudge*." In 561, pp. 91–106.

656 MONOD, Sylvère. "Rebel with a Cause: Hugh of the Maypole." *DiS*, 1(1965):4–26.

BLEAK HOUSE

See 48, 75, 91, 170, 549.*

657 *Bleak House.* Ed. Morton D. Zabel. Boston: Houghton Mifflin, 1956.†

658 KORG, Jacob, ed. *Bleak House: A Collection of Critical Essays.* TCI. Englewood Cliffs, N.J.: Prentice-Hall, 1968.†

659 AXTON, William. "The Trouble with Esther." *MLQ,* 27(1965):545-57.

660 BUTT, John. "*Bleak House* in the Context of 1851." In 571.*

661 CRAIG, David. "Fiction and the Rising Industrial Classes." *EIC,* 17(1967):64-73.

662 CROMPTON, Louis. "Satire and Symbolism in *Bleak House.*" *NCF,* 12(1958):284-303.

663 DELESPINASSE, Doris Stringham. "The Significance of Dual Point of View in *Bleak House.*" NCF, 23(1968):253-64.

664 DONOVAN, Robert Alan. In 58, pp. 206-37.*

665 FORD, George H. "Self-Help and the Helpless in *Bleak House.*" In 88, pp. 92-105.*

666 FRADIN, Joseph I. "Will and Society in *Bleak House.*" *PMLA,* 81(1966):95-109.

667 FRIEDMAN, Norman. "The Shadow and the Sun." *BUSE,* 3(1957):147-66.

668 GRENANDER, M. E. "The Mystery and the Moral: Point of View in Dickens's *Bleak House.*" *NCF,* 10(1956):301-5.

669 GUERARD, Albert J. "*Bleak House:* Structure and Style." *SoR,* 5(1969):332-49.

670 HAIGHT, Gordon. "Dickens and Lewis on Spontaneous Combustion." *NCF,* 10(1955):53-63.

671 HARVEY, W. J. "Chance and Design in *Bleak House.*" In 561, pp. 145-57.*

672 STONE, Harry. "Charles Dickens and Harriet Beecher Stowe." *NCF,* 12(1957):188-202.

673 SUCKSMITH, H. P. "Dickens at Work on *Bleak House:* His Memoranda and Number-Plans." *RMS,* 9(1965):47-85.

674 ZABEL, Morton D. Introductions to *Bleak House* and *A Tale of Two Cities.* In 449.

DAVID COPPERFIELD

675 *David Copperfield.* Ed. George Ford. Boston: Houghton Mifflin, 1958.†

676 BROWN, E. K. "David Copperfield." *YR,* 37(1948):651-66.

677 COLLINS, Philip. "*David Copperfield* and East Anglia." *Dickensian,* 61(1965):46-51.

678 FIELDING, K. J. "The Making of *David Copperfield.*" *Listener,* July 19, 1951:93-5.

679 JONES, John. "*David Copperfield.*" In 561, pp. 133-43.

680 KETTLE, Arnold. "Thoughts on *David Copperfield.*" *REL*, 2(1961):65–74.

681 KINCAID, James R. "Dickens' Subversive Humor: *David Copperfield.*" *NCF*, 22(1968):313–29.

682 KINCAID, James R. "The Structure of *David Copperfield.*" *DiS*, 2(1966):74–95.

683 MARSHALL, William H. "The Image of Steerforth and the Structure of *David Copperfield.*" *TSLL*, 5(1960):57–65.

684 NEEDHAM, Gwendolyn B. "The Undisciplined Heart of David Copperfield." *NCF*, 9(1955):81–107.

685 ODDIE, William. "Mr. Micawber and the Redefinition of Experience." *Dickensian*, 63(1967):100–9.

686 SPILKA, Mark. "*David Copperfield* as Psychological Fiction." *CritQ*, 1(1959):292–301. See also his 637.

687 STRONG, Leonard A. G. *Personal Remarks.* London: Neville, 1953, pp. 103–22.

688 TEDLOCK, E. W., Jr. "Kafka's Imitation of *David Copperfield.*" *CL*, 7(1955):52–62.

689 WOOLF, Virginia. "*David Copperfield.*" *The Moment and Other Essays.* London: Hogarth, 1947.

DOMBEY AND SON

690 AXTON, William. "*Dombey and Son:* From Stereotype to Archetype." *ELH*, 31(1964):301–17.

691 AXTON, William. "Tonal Unity in *Dombey and Son.*" *PMLA*, 78(1963):341–8.

692 COLLINS, Philip. "*Dombey and Son*—Then and Now." *Dickensian*, 63(1967):82–94.

693 LEAVIS, F. R. "*Dombey and Son.*" *SR*, 70(1962):177–201.*

694 LUCAS, John. "Dickens and *Dombey and Son:* Past and Present Imperfect." David B. Howard et al., eds., *Tradition and Tolerance in Nineteenth-Century Fiction.* See 119.

695 MOYNAHAN, Julian. "Dealings with the Firm of Dombey and Son: Firmness versus Wetness." In 561, pp. 121–31.

696 STONE, Harry. "Dickens and Leitmotif: Music-Staircase Imagery in *Dombey and Son.*" *CE*, 25(1963):217–20.

697 STONE, Harry. "The Novel as Fairy Tale: Dickens' *Dombey and Son.*" *ES*, 47(1966):1–27.

698 TILLOTSON, Kathleen. In 97, pp. 157–201.*

699 TILLOTSON, Kathleen. "New Readings in *Dombey and Son.*" In *Imagined Worlds: Essays on Some English Novels and Novelists in Honor of John Butt.* Eds. Maynard Mack and Ian Gregor. London: Methuen, 1968, pp. 172–82.

EDWIN DROOD

700 *Edwin Drood.* Ed. J. I. M. Stewart. London: Lehmann, 1950.

701 AYLMER, Felix. *The Drood Case.* London: Hart-Davis, 1964.

702 BAKER, Richard M. *The Drood Murder Case: Five Studies in Dickens's* Edwin Drood. Berkeley: U of California P, 1951.

703 COCKSHUT, A. O. J. "*Edwin Drood:* Early and Late Dickens Reconciled." In 561, pp. 227-238.

704 COX, A. J. "The Drood Remains." *DiS,* 2(1966):33-44. (On the manuscript.)

705 FORD, George H. "Dickens's Notebook and *Edwin Drood.*" *NCF,* 6(1952):275-80.

706 MITCHELL, Charles. "*The Mystery of Edwin Drood:* The Interior and Exterior of Self." *ELH,* 33(1966):228-46.

707 PRITCHETT, V. S. "*Edwin Drood.*" In 87, pp. 83-8.*

708 WALTERS, J. Cuming. *The Complete* Edwin Drood: *Full Text with the History, Combinations and Solutions 1870-1912.* London: Chapman & Hall, 1912.

GREAT EXPECTATIONS

709 *Great Expectations.* Ed. with introduction and notes by Louis Crompton. Indianapolis: Bobbs-Merrill, 1964.†*

710 BARNES, John. *Dickens:* Great Expectations. London: Macmillan, 1966. (Study and reprint of criticism.)

711 CONNOLLY, Thomas E. "Technique in *Great Expectations.*" *PQ,* 34(1955):48-55.

712 FIELDING, K. J. "The Critical Autonomy of *Great Expectations.*" *REL,* 2(1961):75-88.

713 FORKER, Charles R. "The Language of Hands in *Great Expectations.*" *TSLL,* 3(1961):280-93.

714 FRIEDMAN, Norman. "Versions of Form in Fiction—*Great Expectations* and *The Great Gatsby.*" *Accent,* 14(1954):246-64.

715 HAGAN, John H., Jr. "The Poor Labyrinth: The Theme of Social Injustice in Dickens' *Great Expectations.*" *NCF,* 9(1954):169-78.

716 HAGAN, John H., Jr. "Structural Patterns in Dickens' *Great Expectations.*" *ELH,* 21(1954):54-66.

717 HARDY, Barbara. "Food and Ceremony in *Great Expectations.*" *EIC,* 13(1963):351-63.

718 HOUSE, Humphry. In 608, pp. 201-20.

719 HYNES, Joseph A. "Image and Symbol in *Great Expectations.*" *ELH,* 30(1963):258-92.

720 LETTIS, Richard, and William E. MORRIS, eds. *Assessing* Great Expectations. San Francisco: Chandler, 1963. (Anthology of criticism.)†*

721 LEVINE, George. "Communication in *Great Expectations*." *NCF*, 18(1964):175–81.

722 MARCUS, Phillip L. "Theme and Suspense in the Plot of *Great Expectations*." *DiS*, 2(1966):57–73.

723 MEISEL, Martin. "Miss Havisham Brought to Book." *PMLA*, 81(1966):278–85.

724 MOYNAHAN, Julian. "The Hero's Guilt: The Case of *Great Expectations*." *EIC*, 10(1960):60–79.

725 NISBET, Ada. "The Autobiographical Matrix of *Great Expectations*." *VN*, 15(1959):10–13.

726 RICKS, Christopher. "*Great Expectations*." In 561, pp. 199–211.*

727 SHAW, George Bernard. "*Great Expectations*." Van Wyck Brooks et al., *A Book of Prefaces*. New York: Limited Editions Club, 1949, 29–43.

728 SPILKA, Mark. "*Great Expectations*: A Kafkan Reading." In 93, pp. 103–24.

729 STANGE, G. Robert. "Expectations Well Lost: Dickens' Fable for His Time." *CE*, 16(1954):9–17.

730 STONE, Harry. "Fire, Hand, and Gate: Dickens' *Great Expectations*." *KR*, 24(1962):662–91.*

731 THOMAS, R. George. *Charles Dickens:* Great Expectations. SEngL. London: Arnold, 1964.

732 VAN GHENT, Dorothy. See 98, pp. 125–138,* and 753.

733 VANDE KEIFT, Ruth M. "Patterns of Communication in *Great Expectations*." *NCF*, 15(1961):325–34.

734 WENTERSDORF, Karl P. "Mirror Images in *Great Expectations*." *NCF*, 21(1966):203–24.

HARD TIMES

See 72,* 170, 561, 582.

735 *Hard Times*. Ed. George Ford and Sylvère Monod. New York: Norton, 1966.†*

736 GRAY, Paul E., ed. Hard Times: *A Collection of Critical Essays*. TCI. Englewood Cliffs, N.J.: Prentice-Hall, 1969.

737 CARNALL, Geoffrey. "Dickens, Mrs. Gaskell and the Preston Strike." *VS*, 8(1964):31–48.

738 LODGE, David. "The Rhetoric of *Hard Times*." In 74, pp. 144–63.

739 SHAW, George Bernard. Introduction to *Hard Times*. London: Waverley, 1910.

740 WALDOCK, A. J. A. "The Status of *Hard Times*." *Southerly*, 9(1948):33–9.

741 WILLIAMS, Raymond. Introduction to *Hard Times*. New York: Fawcett, 1966.† Also in 136, ch. 5.

Little Dorrit

See 561, 582.

742 BUTT, John. "The Topicality of *Little Dorrit*." *UTQ*, 29(1959):1-11.

743 HERNING, P. D. "Dickens's Monthly Number-Plans for *Little Dorrit*." *MP*, 64(1966):22-63.

744 MC MASTER, R. D. "*Little Dorrit*: Experience and Design." *QQ*, 67(1961):530-8.

745 REID, John C. *Charles Dickens: Little Dorrit*. London: Arnold, 1967.†

746 TRILLING, Lionel. "Little Dorrit." *The Opposing Self; Nine Essays in Criticism*. New York: Viking, 1955, pp. 50-65.†

747 WILDE, Alan. "Mr. F's Aunt and the Analogical Structure of *Little Dorrit*." *NCF*, 20(1965):33-44.

Martin Chuzzlewit

748 BENJAMIN, Edwin B. "The Structure of *Martin Chuzzlewit*." *PQ*, 34(1955):39-47.

749 DYSON, A. E. "*Martin Chuzzlewit*: Howls the Sublime." *CritQ*, 9(1967):234-53.

750 HARDY, Barbara. "*Martin Chuzzlewit*." In 561, pp. 107-20.

751 NISBET, Ada. "The Mystery of 'Martin Chuzzlewit.'" *Essays Critical and Historical Dedicated to Lily B. Campbell*. Berkeley: U of California P, 1950.*

752 STONE, Harry. "Dickens' Use of His American Experiences in *Martin Chuzzlewit*." *PMLA*, 72(1957):464-78.

753 VAN GHENT, Dorothy. "The Dickens World: The View from Todger's." *SR*, 58(1950):419-38. (Earlier version of 98; largely on *Great Expectations*.)

Nicholas Nickleby

754 CLINTON-BADDELEY, V. C. "Benevolent Teachers of Youth." *Cornhill Mag.*, Autumn 1957:360-82.

755 DARTON, F. J. H. *Vincent Crummles: His Theatre and His Times*. London: Wells, Gardner, Darton, 1926.

The Old Curiosity Shop

756 DYSON, A. E. "*The Old Curiosity Shop*: Innocence and the Grotesque." *CritQ*, 8(1966):111-30.*

757 HUXLEY, Aldous. *Vulgarity in Literature*. London: Chatto & Windus, 1930, 54-9.

Oliver Twist

See 607, 608.

758 *Oliver Twist*. Ed. Kathleen Tillotson. Oxford: Clarendon P, 1966. (First vol. in the Clarendon Dickens.)*

759 *Oliver Twist.* Ed. Peter Fairclough; introduction by Angus Wilson. London: Penguin, 1966.†

760 *Oliver Twist.* Ed. J. Hillis Miller. New York: Holt, Rinehart, 1962.†

761 BISHOP, Jonathan. "The Hero-Villain of *Oliver Twist.*" *VN*, (1959):14–16.

762 BOLL, Ernest. "Charles Dickens in *Oliver Twist.*" *PsyR*, 27(1940):133–43.

763 DUFFY, Joseph M., Jr. "Another Version of Pastoral: *Oliver Twist.*" *ELH*, 35(1968):403–21.

764 EOFF, Sherman. "*Oliver Twist* and the Spanish Picaresque Novel." *SP*, 54(1957):440–7.

765 GRUBB, Gerald G. "On the Serial Publication of *Oliver Twist.*" *MLN*, 56(1941):290–4.

766 HOLLINGSWORTH, Keith. In 173, pp. 111–31.

767 KETTLE, Arnold. In 71, pp. 123–38.*

768 MARCUS, Steven. "Who is Fagin?" *Commentary*, 34(1962):48–59. (Repr. in 619)

769 PRITCHETT, V. S. "*Oliver Twist.*" *Books in General.* New York: Harcourt, Brace, 1953, 191–6.

770 ROSENBERG, Edgar. In 205, pp. 116–37.

771 STONE, Harry. "Dickens and the Jews." *VS*, 2(1959):223–53.*

772 TILLOTSON, Kathleen. "*Oliver Twist.*" *E&S*, 12(1959):87–105.

OUR MUTUAL FRIEND

See 620.

773 BARNARD, Robert. "The Choral Symphony: *Our Mutual Friend.*" *REL*, 2(1961):89–99.

774 BOLL, Ernest. "The Plottings of *Our Mutual Friend.*" *MP*, 42(1944):96–122.

775 JAMES, Henry. Unsigned review of *Our Mutual Friend* in *The Nation*, Dec. 21, 1865. In Henry James, *The Future of the Novel: Essays in the Art of Fiction.* Ed. Leon Edel. New York: Vintage, 1956.†

776 KETTLE, Arnold. "*Our Mutual Friend.*" In 561, pp. 213–25.*

777 MIYOSHI, Masao. "Resolution of Identity in *Our Mutual Friend.*" *VN*, 26(1964):5–9.

778 MONOD, Sylvère. "L'Expression dans *Our Mutual Friend:* manière ou maniérisme?" *EA*, 10(1957):37–48.

779 MORSE, R. "*Our Mutual Friend.*" *PR*, 16(1949):277–89.

780 MUIR, Kenneth. "Image and Structure in *Our Mutual Friend.*" *E&S*, 19(1966):92–105.

THE PICKWICK PAPERS

781 AUDEN, W. H. *The Dyer's Hand.* London: Faber & Faber, 1962, 407–28.*

782 AXTON, William. "Unity and Coherence in *The Pickwick Papers.*" *SEL*, 5(1965):633-76.

783 BEVINGTON, David M. "Seasonal Relevance in *The Pickwick Papers.*" *NCF*, 16(1961):219-30.

784 CHESTERTON, G. K., and F. G. KITTON. *Charles Dickens.* London: Methuen, 1936, pp. 51-71.

785 COLWELL, Mary. "Organization in *Pickwick Papers.*" *DiS*, 3(1967):90-110.

786 DAVIS, Earle. "Dickens and the Evolution of Caricature." *PMLA*, 55(1940):231-40.

787 HARDY, Barbara. "The Triumph of Dingley Dell." *London Review*, (1967):2-11.

788 LANE, Lauriat, Jr. "Mr. Pickwick and *The Dance of Death.*" *NCF*, 14(1959):171-2.

789 MILLER, William, and E. H. STRANGE. *A Centenary Bibliography of the* Pickwick Papers. London: Argonaut, 1936. (Reprints many early reviews.)

Disraeli, Benjamin, Later Earl of Beaconsfield (1804–1881)

NOVELS

790 *Vivian Grey.* London: Colburn, 1826. *The Voyage of Captain Popanilla.* London: Colburn, 1828. *The Young Duke.* London: Colburn & Bentley, 1831. *Contarini Fleming.* London: Murray, 1832. *Ixion in Heaven.* [*Colburn's New Monthly Mag.*, 1832-1834.] London: Bryce, 1853. *The Infernal Marriage.* [*Colburn's New Monthly Mag.*, 1832-1834.] London: Bryce, 1853. *The Wondrous Tale of Alroy.* London: Saunders & Otley, 1833. *Henrietta Temple: A Love Story.* London: Colburn, 1837. *Venetia.* London: Colburn, 1837. *Coningsby: Or the New Generation.* London: Colburn, 1844. *Sybil: Or, The Two Nations.* London: Colburn, 1845. *Tancred: Or the New Crusade.* London: Colburn, 1847. *The Tragedy of Count Alarcos.* London: Bryce, 1853.

791 *Lothair.* London: Longmans, Green, 1870. *Endymion.* London: Longmans, Green, 1880.

BIBLIOGRAPHY

See 25.*

792 SADLEIR, Michael. In 22 and 23.*

COLLECTIONS, LETTERS, ETC.

793 *Bradenham Edition of the Novels and Tales of Benjamin Disraeli.* Introduction by Philip Guedalla. 12 vols. London: Davies, 1926-1927.

794 DISRAELI, Ralph. *Lord Beaconsfield's Correspondence with His Sister, 1832-1852.* London, 1886. Repub. as *Lord Beaconsfield's Letters;* and in 1928 as *Home Letters, Written by Lord Beaconsfield, 1830-1852.*

795   MARCHIONESS OF LONDONDERRY, ed. *Letters of Disraeli to Frances Anne, Marchioness of Londonderry, 1837-1861.* London: Macmillan, 1938.

796   MARQUIS OF ZETLAND, ed. *The Letters of Disraeli to Lady Bradford and Lady Chesterfield.* 2 vols. London: Benn, 1929.

BIOGRAPHICAL AND GENERAL

797   ALDINGTON, Richard. *Four English Portraits.* London: Evans, 1948.

798   BEELEY, Harold. *Disraeli.* London: Duckworth, 1936.

799   BLAKE, Robert. *Disraeli.* London: Eyre & Spottiswoode, 1966.*

800   FROUDE, James Anthony. *Lord Beaconsfield.* New York: Harper, 1890.

801   JERMAN, Bernard R. *The Young Disraeli.* Princeton: Princeton U P, 1960.

802   MAUROIS, André. *Disraeli: A Picture of the Victorian Age.* Trans. Hamish Miles. London: Lane, 1927; New York: Appleton, 1928.

803   MONYPENNY, William Flavelle, and George Earle BUCKLE. *The Life of Benjamin Disraeli.* 6 vols. London: Murray, 1910-1920.*

804   ROTH, Cecil. *Benjamin Disraeli, Earl of Beaconsfield.* New York: Philosophical Library, 1952.

805   STAPLEDON, Sir Reginald George. *Disraeli and the New Age.* London: Faber, 1944.

CRITICAL

See 87, 117,* 124, 170,* 204, 210.

806   ALLEN, Walter. Introduction to *Coningsby.* Chiltern Library Edition. London: Lehmann, 1948.

807   BLAKE, Robert. "Disraeli the Novelist." *EDH,* 34(1966):1-18.

808   BLOOMFIELD, Paul. *Disraeli.* WTW. London and New York: Longmans, Green, 1961.†

809   CHALLEMEL-LACOUR, P. "Le Roman politique en Angleterre." *RDM,* 4(1870):429-50. (On *Lothair.*)

810   CLINE, C. L. "Benjamin Disraeli on the Grotesque in Literature." *RES,* 16(1940):68-71. (On *Vivian Grey.*)

811   CLINE, C. L. "Disraeli and Thackeray." *RES,* 19(1943):404-8.

812   EDELMAN, Maurice. "A Political Novel: Disraeli Sets a Lively Pace." *TLS,* Aug. 7, 1959, pp. x-xi. (On *Coningsby.*)

813   FORBES-BOYD, Eric. "Disraeli the Novelist." *E&S,* n.s.3(1950):100-17.

814   FRIETZSCHE, Arthur H. "Action is Not for Me: Disraeli's Sidonia and the Dream of Power." *Proceedings of the Utah Academy of Sciences, Arts and Letters.* Logan: Utah State U P, 1959-1960. (On *Coningsby.*)

815   FRIETZSCHE, Arthur H. *Disraeli's Religion: The Treatment of Religion in Disraeli's Novels.* Utah State Monograph Series 9, i. Logan: Utah State U P, 1961.

816 FRIETZSCHE, Arthur H. *The Monstrous Clever Young Man: The Novelist Disraeli and His Heroes.* Utah State Monograph Series 7, iii. Logan: Utah State U P, 1959.

817 GARNETT, Richard. "Shelley and Lord Beaconsfield." *Essays of an Ex-Librarian.* London: Heinemann, 1901. (On *Venetia.*)

818 GILBERT, Felix. "The Germany of *Contarini Fleming.*" *ContempR,* 149(1936):74–80.

819 GRAUBARD, Stephen R. "Benjamin Disraeli, the Romantic Egotist." *Burke, Disraeli, Churchill: The Politics of Perseverance.* Cambridge, Mass.: Harvard U P, 1961.

820 GREENE, D. J. "Becky Sharp and Lord Steyne—Thackeray or Disraeli?" *NCF,* 16(1961):157–64.

821 GREY, Rowland. "Disraeli in Fancy Street." *Cornhill Mag.,* n.s.67(1929):102–10. (On *Endymion.*)

822 HAMILTON, Robert. "Disraeli and the Two Nations." *QR,* 288(1950):102–15. (On *Sybil.*)

823 JERMAN, B. R. "Disraeli's Audience." *SAQ,* 55(1956):463–72.

824 KIRK, Russell. "The Social Imagination of Disraeli." *QQ,* 59(1952):471–85.

825 LEVINE, Richard A. *Benjamin Disraeli.* TEAS. New York: Twayne, 1968.

826 MASEFIELD, Muriel. *Peacocks and Primroses: A Survey of Disraeli's Novels.* London: Bles, 1953.*

827 MODDER, Montague. "The Alien Patriot in Disraeli's Novels." *LQHR,* 159(1934):363–72.

828 PAINTING, David E. "Thackeray *v.* Disraeli." *QR,* 302(1964):396–407.

829 SHERMAN, Stuart P. "The Disraelian Irony." *Points of View.* New York and London: Scribner's, 1924.

830 STEPHEN, Leslie. "Mr. Disraeli's Novels." *Hours in a Library; Second Series.* London: Smith, Elder, 1876.*

831 STEVENSON, Lionel. "Stepfathers of Victorianism." *VQR,* 6(1930):251–67.

832 STEWART, R. W. "The Publication and Reception of Disraeli's *Vivian Grey.*" *QR,* 218(1960):409–17.

833 SWINNERTON, Frank. "Disraeli as a Novelist." *YR,* n.s.17(1928):283–300.

Du Maurier, George (1834–1896)

MAIN NOVELS

834 *Peter Ibbetson.* 2 vols. 1892. *Trilby.* 3 vols. 1894. *The Martian: A Novel,* 1897.

STUDIES

835 DU MAURIER, Daphne. *The Du Mauriers.* New York: Doubleday, 1937.

836 DU MAURIER, Daphne, ed. *The Young George Du Maurier: A Selection of His Letters, 1860-1867*. Garden City, N.Y.: Doubleday, 1952.

837 STEVENSON, Lionel. "George Du Maurier and the Romantic Novel." *EDH*, 30(1960):36-54.

838 WHITELEY, D. P. *Du Maurier: His Life and Work*. New York: Pellegrini, 1948.

839 WOOD, T. M. *Du Maurier, the Satirist of the Victorians*. London: Chatto & Windus, 1913.

Eden, Emily (1797-1869)

MAIN NOVELS

840 *Portraits of the People*, 1844. *The Semi-Attached Couple*, 1860. *Up the Country*, 1866.

Egan, Pierce (1772-1849)

MAIN NOVELS

841 *Life in London, or the Day and Night Scenes of Jerry Hawthorn, Esq. and Corinthian Tom*, 1821. *The Life of an Actor*, 1825. *Finish to the Adventures of Tom, Jerry and Logic in their Pursuits through Life In and Out of London*, 1828.

"Eliot, George" (Mary Ann Evans Cross) (1819-1880)

NOVELS

842 *Scenes of Clerical Life*. [In *Blackwood's* as "The Sad Fortune of the Rev. Amos Barton," "Mr. Gilfil's Love Story," and "Janet's Repentance." Jan.-Nov. 1857.] 2 vols. Edinburgh: Blackwood, 1858. *Adam Bede*. 3 vols. Edinburgh: Blackwood, 1859. *The Mill on the Floss*. 3 vols. Edinburgh and London: Blackwood, 1860. *Silas Marner: The Weaver of Raveloe*. Edinburgh and London: Blackwood, 1861. *Romola*. [*Cornhill Mag.*, July 1862-Aug. 1863.] 3 vols. London: Smith, Elder, 1863. *Felix Holt the Radical*. 3 vols. Edinburgh and London: Blackwood, 1866. *Middlemarch, a Study of Provincial Life*. [First pub. by Blackwood in 8 nos., Dec. 1871-Dec. 1872.] 4 vols. Edinburgh: Blackwood, 1872. *Daniel Deronda*. 4 vols. Edinburgh and London: Blackwood, 1876.

BIBLIOGRAPHY AND REFERENCE

See 25.* A complete bibliography is in progress.

843 BARRY, J. D. "The Literary Reputation of George Eliot's Fiction." *BB*, 22(1950):176-82.

844 HAIGHT, Gordon S. *A Century of George Eliot Criticism*. Boston: Houghton Mifflin, 1965.*†

845 HAIGHT, Gordon S. "The George Eliot and George Henry Lewes Collection." *YULG*, 35(1961):170-1.

846 HAIGHT, Gordon S. "The Tinker Collection of George Eliot Manuscripts." *YULG*, 29(1955):148-50.

847 MUDGE, I. G., and M. E. SEARS. *A George Eliot Dictionary*. London: Routledge; New York: Wilson, 1924.

848 STANG, R., ed. *Discussions of George Eliot*. Boston: Heath, 1960.†

TEXTS

No complete edition. A critical edition of the novels is in progress.

849 *The Cabinet Edition*. 20 vols. Edinburgh and London: Blackwood, 1878-1885.

850 *The Writings of George Eliot*. The Warwickshire Edition. 25 vols. Boston and New York: Houghton Mifflin, 1908. (Includes the authorized *Life, Letters, and Journals* by J. W. Cross.)

851 CROSS, J. W. *George Eliot's Life as Related in Her Letters and Journals*. New York: Harper, 1885; Boston and New York: Crowell, 1900, 1904.

852 HAIGHT, Gordon S. *The George Eliot Letters*. 7 vols. New Haven: Yale U P, 1954-1955.*

853 PINNEY, Thomas, ed. *Essays of George Eliot*. London: Routledge & Kegan Paul, 1963.

854 PINNEY, Thomas. "More Leaves from George Eliot's Notebook." *HLQ*, 29(1966):353-76.

BIOGRAPHICAL AND GENERAL

855 BENNETT, Joan. *George Eliot: Her Mind and Art*. Cambridge: Cambridge U P, 1948, 1962. (Useful general survey.)*†

856 BULLETT, Gerald. *George Eliot*. London: Collins, 1947. Pub. as *George Eliot: Her Life and Books*. New Haven: Yale U P, 1948.

857 COUCH, John P. *George Eliot in France: A French Appraisal of George Eliot's Writings, 1858-1960*. UNCSCL 41. Chapel Hill: U of North Carolina P, 1967.

858 DEAKIN, Mary H. *The Early Life of George Eliot*. Manchester, Eng.: Manchester U P, 1913.

859 HAIGHT, Gordon S. *George Eliot: A Biography*. New York and Oxford: Oxford U P, 1968.*

860 HAIGHT, Gordon S. *George Eliot and John Chapman*. New Haven: Yale U P, 1940. [2d ed., Hamden, Conn.: Archon, 1969]*

861 HANSON, Lawrence, and Elizabeth M. HANSON. *Marian Evans and George Eliot*. London: Oxford U P, 1952. (Unreliable but very readable.)

862 MC KENZIE, K. A. *Edith Simcox and George Eliot*. Introduction by Gordon S. Haight. London: Oxford U P, 1961.

863 MAHEU, P. G. *La Pensée religieuse et morale de George Eliot.* Paris: Didier, 1959.

864 SPEAIGHT, Robert. *George Eliot.* New York: Roy, 1954.

865 STEPHEN, Leslie. *George Eliot.* London: Macmillan, 1902.*

CRITICAL AND OTHER STUDIES

See 52,* 72,* 87,* 95,* 117,* 135,* 171,* 389.*

866 HAIGHT, Gordon S., ed. *A Century of George Eliot Criticism.* London: Methuen, 1966.*

867 ADAM, Ian W. "Character and Destiny in George Eliot's Fiction." *NCF,* 20(1965):127-43.

868 ALLEN, Walter. *George Eliot.* New York: Macmillan, 1964.†

869 ALLOTT, Miriam. "George Eliot in the 1860's." *VS,* 5(1961):93-108.

870 BETHELL, S. L. "The Novels of George Eliot." *Criterion,* 18(1938):39-57.

871 BISSELL, C. T. "Social Analysis in the Novels of George Eliot." *ELH,* 18(1951):221-39.

872 BISSON, L. A. "Proust, Bergson and George Eliot." *MLR,* 40(1945):104-14.

873 BOURL'HONNE, P. *George Eliot: Essai de biographie intellectuelle et morale, 1819-1854.* Paris: Champion, 1933.

874 CARROLL, D. R. "An Image of Disenchantment in the Novels of George Eliot." *RES,* 11(1960):29-41.

875 CASEY, W. "George Eliot's Theory of Fiction." *WVUPP,* 9(1953):20-32.

876 FELTES, N. N. "George Eliot and the Unified Sensibility." *PMLA,* 79(1964):130-6.

877 GARY, Franklin. "In Search of George Eliot: An Approach through Marcel Proust." *Symposium,* 4(1933):186-206.

878 HAIGHT, Gordon S. "George Eliot's Originals." In 88, pp. 177-93.*

879 HAIGHT, Gordon S. "George Eliot's Theory of Fiction." *VN,* 10(1957):1-3.

880 HARDY, Barbara. *The Novels of George Eliot: A Study in Form.* London: Athlone, 1959.*†

881 HARVEY, W. J. *The Art of George Eliot.* London: Chatto & Windus, 1961.*

882 HARVEY, W. J. "George Eliot and the Omniscient Author Convention." *NCF,* 12(1958):81-108.

883 HOUGH, Graham. "Novelist-Philosopher: George Eliot." *Horizon,* 17(1948):50-61.

884 HOUSE, Humphry. "Qualities of George Eliot's Unbelief." *All in Due Time.* London: Hart-Davis, 1955.*

885 HUTTON, Richard Holt. "George Eliot." *Essays in Literary Criticism.* Philadelphia: 1876, pp. 227-300.

886 HYDE, W. J. "George Eliot and the Climate of Realism." *PMLA*, 72(1957):147-64.

887 JAMES, Henry. "Novels of George Eliot." *Atlantic Monthly*, 18(1866):479-92.* (James wrote much about George Eliot in reviews, letters, and in his autobiographical *The Middle Years;* see Henry James, *Literary Reviews and Essays.* Ed. Albert Mordell. New York: Grove, 1957, pp. 387-90.)†

888 KAMINSKY, A. R. "George Eliot, George Henry Lewes and the Novel." *PMLA*, 70(1955):997-1013.

889 KNOEPFLMACHER, U. C. *George Eliot's Early Novels: The Limits of Realism.* Berkeley and Los Angeles: U. of California P, 1968.

890 KNOEPFLMACHER, U. C. "George Eliot: The Search for a Religious Tradition." In 187, pp. 24-71.*

891 LEVINE, George. "Determinism and Responsibility in the Works of George Eliot." *PMLA*, 77(1962):268-79.*

892 MANSELL, Darrell, Jr. "Ruskin and George Eliot's 'Realism.' " *Criticism*, 7(1965):203-16.

893 MILNER, Ian. "George Eliot and the Limits of Victorian Realism." *PP*, 6(1963):48-59.

894 NAUMAN, W. "The Architecture of George Eliot's Novels." *MLQ*, 9(1948):37-50.

895 O'BRIEN, Kate. "George Eliot: A Moralizing Fabulist." *EDH*, 27(1955):34-46.

896 PARIS, Bernard J. *Experiments in Life: George Eliot's Quest for Values.* Detroit: Wayne State U P, 1965.

897 PARLETT, M. "The Influence of Contemporary Criticism on George Eliot." *SP*, 30(1933):103-32.

898 RENDALL, Vernon. "George Eliot and the Classics." *N&Q*, 192(1947):544-6, 564-5; 193(1948):148-9, 272-4.

899 RUST, J. D. "The Art of Fiction in George Eliot's Reviews." *RES*, 7(1956):164-72.

900 SACKVILLE-WEST, Vita. "George Eliot." In 79, 1:187-195.

901 SIMON, Irène. "Innocence in the Novels of George Eliot." *English Studies Today.* Ed. G. A. Bonnard. Bern: Franke, 1961.

902 STUMP, Reva. *Movement and Vision in George Eliot's Novels.* Seattle: U of Washington P, 1959.

903 SVAGLIC, M. J. "Religion in the Novels of George Eliot." *JEGP*, 53(1954):145-59.

904 THALE, Jerome. *The Novels of George Eliot.* New York: Columbia U P, 1959.*

905 THOMSON, Patricia. "The Three Georges." *NCF*, 18(1963):137-50. (On Eliot, George Sand, and G. H. Lewes.)

906 WOOLF, Virginia. "George Eliot." *TLS*, 18(1919):657-8. Repr. in *The Common Reader, First Series* (1925).†

907 WORTH, George J. "The Intruder in George Eliot's Fiction." *Six Studies in Nineteenth-Century English Literature and Thought.* Ed. Harold Orel and George J. Worth. *UKPHS* 35. Lawrence: U of Kansas P, 1962.

ADAM BEDE

See 98.*

908 CREEGER, G. R. "An Interpretation of *Adam Bede.*" *ELH*, 23(1956):218-38.

909 DENEAU, D. P. "Inconsistencies and Inaccuracies in *Adam Bede.*" *NCF*, 14(1959):71-5.

910 DIEKHOFF, J. S. "The Happy Ending of *Adam Bede.*" *ELH*, 3(1936):221-7.

911 FOAKES, R. A. "*Adam Bede* Reconsidered." *English*, 12(1959):173-6.

912 FYFE, A. J. "The Interpretation of *Adam Bede.*" *NCF*, 9(1954):134-9.

913 GREGOR, Ian. "The Two Worlds of *Adam Bede.*" Ian Gregor and Brian Nicholas, *The Moral and the Story.* London: Faber, 1962.*

914 HARVEY, W. J. "The Treatment of Time in Adam Bede." *Anglia*, 75(1957):429-40.

915 HUSSEY, M. "Structure and Imagery in *Adam Bede.*" *NCF*, 10(1955):115-29.*

916 PATERSON, John. Introduction to *Adam Bede.* Boston: Houghton Mifflin, 1968.†

DANIEL DERONDA

See 187,* 205.*

917 BEATY, Jerome. "*Daniel Deronda* and the Question of Unity in Fiction." *VN*, 15(1959):16-20.

918 BEEBE, M. " 'Visions Are Creators': The Unity of *Daniel Deronda.*" *BUSE*, 1(1955):166-77.

919 CARROLL, David R. "The Unity of *Daniel Deronda.*" *EIC*, 9(1959):369-80.

920 CIRILLO, Albert R. "Salvation in *Daniel Deronda:* The Fortunate Overthrow of Gwendolen Harleth." *LitM*, 1(1967):203-43, 315-18.

921 JAMES, Henry. "*Daniel Deronda:* A Conversation." *Atlantic Monthly*, 38(1876):684-94. Repr. in 72, pp. 79-125.*

922 KNOEPFLMACHER, U. C. "*Daniel Deronda* and Shakespeare." *VN*, 19(1961):27-8.

923 LEAVIS, F. R. "George Eliot's Zionist Novel." *Commentary*, 30(1960):317-25. [Repr. as introduction to *Daniel Deronda.* New York: Harper, 1961.]†

924 PREYER, Robert. "Beyond the Liberal Imagination; Vision and Unreality in *Daniel Deronda.*" *VS*, 4(1960):33-54.

925 ROBINSON, Carole. "The Severe Angel: A Study of *Daniel Deronda.*" *ELH*, 31(1964):278-300.

926 THALE, Jerome. "*Daniel Deronda:* The Darkened World." *MFS*, 3(1957):227-34.

927 THALE, Jerome. "River Imagery in *Daniel Deronda*." *NCF*, 8(1954):300-6.

FELIX HOLT

See 136,* 210.

928 CARROLL, David R. "*Felix Holt:* Society as Protagonist." *NCF*, 18(1962):237-52.

929 MYERS, W. E. "Politics and Personality in *Felix Holt*." *RMS*, 10(1966):5-33.

930 THOMSON, Fred C. "*Felix Holt* as Classic Tragedy." *NCF*, 16(1961):47-58.

931 THOMSON, Fred C. "The Genesis of *Felix Holt*." *PMLA*, 74(1959):576-84.

MIDDLEMARCH

See 48, 71,* 187,* 191, 389.*

932 *Middlemarch*. Ed. Gordon S. Haight. Boston: Houghton Mifflin, 1956.†

933 ANDERSON, Quentin. "George Eliot in *Middlemarch*." See 39, pp. 274-93.*

934 BEATY, Jerome. "The Forgotten Past of Will Ladislaw." *NCF*, 13(1958):159-63.

935 BEATY, Jerome. "History by Indirection: The Era of Reform in *Middlemarch*." *VS*, (1957):173-9.

936 BEATY, Jerome. *Middlemarch from Notebook to Novel: A Study of George Eliot's Creative Method*. Urbana: U of Illinois P, 1960.*

937 BEDIENT, Calvin. "*Middlemarch:* Touching Down." *HudR*, 22(1969):70-84.

938 CARROLL, David R. "Unity through Analogy: An Interpretation of *Middlemarch*." *VS*, 2(1959):305-16.

939 DAICHES, David. *George Eliot: Middlemarch*. SEngL. London: Arnold, 1963.†

940 FERNANDO, Lloyd. "George Eliot, Feminism, and Dorothea Brooke." *REL*, 4(1963):76-90.

941 FERRIS, Sumner J. "*Middlemarch:* George Eliot's Masterpiece." In 88, pp. 194-207.*

942 GREENBERG, Robert A. "The Heritage of Will Ladislaw." *NCF*, 15(1961):355-8. (One of several answers to 934.)

943 HAGAN, J. "*Middlemarch:* Narrative Unity in the Story of Dorothea Brooke." *NCF*, 16(1961):17-31.

944 ISAACS, Neil D. "*Middlemarch:* Crescendo of Obligatory Drama." *NCF*, 18(1963):21-34.

945 JAMES, Henry. Unsigned review of *Middlemarch*, in *The Galaxy*, March, 1873. [Repr. Henry James, *The Future of the Novel: Essays in the Art of Fiction*. Ed. Leon Edel. New York: Vintage, 1956, pp. 80-89.] See also 887.*†

946 KITCHEL, A. T., ed. *Quarry for Middlemarch*. Berkeley: U of California P, 1950.*

947 LEAVIS, F. R. See 72.*

948   LERNER, L. D. "The Cool Gaze and the Warm Heart." *Listener*, 64(1960):518-19, 522.

949   LUECKE, Sister Jane Marie. "Ladislaw and the *Middlemarch* Vision." *NCF*, 19(1964):55-64.

950   STALLKNECHT, Newton P. "Resolution and Independence: A Reading of *Middlemarch*." In 93, pp. 125-52.

951   STEINER, F. G. "A Preface to *Middlemarch*." *NCF*, 9(1955):262-79.

THE MILL ON THE FLOSS

952   *The Mill on the Floss*. Ed. Gordon S. Haight. Boston: Houghton Mifflin, 1961.†

953   LEE, R. H. "The Unity of *The Mill on the Floss*." *ESA*, 7(1964):34-53.

954   LEVINE, George. "Intelligence as Deception: *The Mill on the Floss*." *PMLA*, 80(1965):402-9.

955   MILNER, Ian. "The Quest for Community in *The Mill on the Floss*." Prague Studies in English XII. Prague: U of Karlova, 1968, pp. 77-92.

956   PARIS, Bernard J. "The Inner Conflicts of Maggie Tulliver: A Horneyan Analysis." *CentR*, 13(1969):166-99.

957   PARIS, Bernard J. "Towards a Revaluation of George Eliot's *The Mill on the Floss*." *NCF*, 11(1956):18-31.

958   STEINHOFF, W. R. "Intention and Fulfillment in the Ending of *The Mill on the Floss*." *The Image of the Work*, by B. H. Lehman et al. *UCPES* 11. Berkeley: U of California P, 1955, pp. 23-51.

959   THALE, Jerome. "Image and Theme: *The Mill on the Floss*." *UKCR*, 23(1957):227-34.

960   WELSH, A. "George Eliot and the Romance." *NCF*, 14(1959):241-54.

ROMOLA

961   HUZZARD, J. A. "The Treatment of Florence and Florentine Characters in George Eliot's *Romola*." *Italica*, 34(1957):158-65.

962   ROBINSON, Carole. "*Romola*: A Reading of the Novel." *VS*, 6(1962):29-42.

963   TOSELLO, Maria. *Le Fonti Italiane della* Romola *di George Eliot*. Torino: Giappichelli, 1956. (On the sources.)

SCENES OF CLERICAL LIFE

964   DENEAU, Daniel P. "A Note on George Eliot's 'Amos Barton': Reticence and Chronology." *N&S*, n.s.6(1959):450-1.

965   KNOEPFLMACHER, U. C. "George Eliot's Anti-Romantic Romance: 'Mrs. Gilfil's Love Story.'" *VN*, 31(1967):11-15.

966   NOBLE, Thomas A. *George Eliot's Scenes of Clerical Life*. New Haven: Yale U P, 1965.

SILAS MARNER

967 CARROLL, David R. "*Silas Marner:* Reversing the Oracles of Religion." *LitM*, 1(1967):165-200.*

968 HEILMAN, R. B. "Return to Raveloe." *EJ*, 46(1957):1-10.

969 THALE, Jerome. "George Eliot's Fable for Her Times." *CE*, 19(1958):141-6. (Expanded version as introduction to Holt, Rinehart edition of *Silas Marner.*)*†

970 THOMSON, Fred C. "The Theme of Alienation in *Silas Marner.*" *NCF*, 20(1965):69-84.

"Farrar, Dean" (Farrar, Frederick William) (1831-1903)

MAIN NOVELS

971 *Eric, or Little by Little. A Tale of Roslyn School.* Edinburgh, 1858. *St. Winifred's, or The World of School*, 1862. *Gathering Clouds. A Tale of the Days of St. Chrysostom.* 2 vols., 1895.

972 FARRAR, R. *The Life of Frederick William Farrar.* 1904.

Ferrier, Susan Edmondstone (1782-1854)

973 *Marriage, A Novel.* 3 vols. 1818. *The Inheritance.* 3 vols. 1824. *Destiny, or the Chief's Daughter.* 3 vols. 1831. *Works.* 4 vols. 1928. (Includes her three novels and a memoir by J. A. Doyle.)

STUDIES

974 BUSHNELL, Nelson S. "Susan Ferrier's *Marriage* as a Novel of Manners." *SSL*, 5(1968):216-28.

975 GRANT, Aline. *Susan Ferrier of Edinburgh: A Biography.* Denver: Swallow, 1957.

976 PARKER, W. M. *Susan Ferrier and John Galt.* London: Longmans, Green, 1965.

Galt, John (1779-1839)

MAIN NOVELS

977 *The Ayrshire Legatees; or The Pringle Family*, 1821. *Annals of the Parish, or The Chronicle of Dalmailing, during the Ministry of the Rev. Micah Balwhidder*, 1821. *The Provost*, 1822. *The Entail; or, The Lairds of Grippy.* 3 vols. 1823. *The Last of the Lairds; or, The Life and Opinions of Malachi Mailings, Esq. of Auldbiggings*, 1826. *Lawrie Todd; or The Settlers in the Woods.* 3 vols. 1830. *Bogle Corbet, or The Emigrants.* 3 vols. 1831.

978 *Works.* Ed. D. S. Meldrum and W. Roughead. 10 vols. Edinburgh: Grant, 1936.

STUDIES

979 ABERDEIN, J. W. *John Galt.* Oxford: Oxford U P, 1936.

980 BOOTH, Bradford A. "A Bibliography of John Galt." *BB*, 16(1936):7–9.

981 BOOTH, Bradford A. "John Galt: A Study in Scottish Vernacular Fiction." Introduction to Galt's *The Gathering of the West.* Baltimore: Johns Hopkins U P, 1939.

982 GORDON, R. K. *John Galt.* Toronto: Oxford U P, 1920.

983 LYELL, Frank Hallam. *A Study of the Novels of John Galt.* Princeton: Princeton U P, 1942.

Gaskell, Elizabeth Cleghorn, née Stevenson (1810–1865)

NOVELS

984 *Mary Barton, a Tale of Manchester Life.* 2 vols. London: Chapman & Hall, 1848. *Ruth.* 3 vols. London: Chapman & Hall, 1853. *Cranford.* [*Household Words*, Dec. 13, 1851–May 21, 1853.] London: Chapman & Hall, 1853. *North and South.* [*Household Words*, Sept. 2, 1854–Jan. 27, 1855.] 2 vols. London: Chapman & Hall, 1855. *Sylvia's Lovers.* 3 vols. London: Smith, Elder, 1863. *Wives and Daughters. An Every-Day Story.* 2 vols. London: Smith, Elder, 1866.

BIBLIOGRAPHIES

See 25.*

985 NORTHUP, Clark S. Bibliographical appendage to Gerald Dewitt Sanders's *Elizabeth Gaskell. CSE* 15. New Haven: Yale U P, 1929.

986 SADLEIR, Michael. In 22.

COLLECTIONS, LETTERS

987 *The Works of Mrs. Gaskell.* Knutsford Edition. Ed. A. W. Ward. 8 vols. London: Smith, Elder, 1906–1911.

988 *The Novels and Tales of Mrs. Gaskell.* World's Classics Edition. Ed. Clement Shorter. 11 vols. Oxford: Oxford U P, 1906–1919.

989 CHAPPLE, J. A. V., and Arthur POLLARD, eds. *The Letters of Mrs. Gaskell.* Cambridge, Mass.: Harvard U P, 1967.*

990 POLLARD, Arthur. "Mrs. Gaskell's Life of Charlotte Brontë." *BJRL*, 47(1965):453–88. (Contains appendix on some new Gaskell letters by Albert H. Preston.)

991 WHITEHALL, Jane, ed. *Letters of Mrs. Gaskell and Charles Eliot Norton, 1855–1865.* London: Oxford U P, 1932.

BIOGRAPHICAL AND GENERAL

See 142, 162.

992 ALLOTT, Miriam. *Elizabeth Gaskell*. WTW. London and New York: Longmans, Green, 1960.†

993 FFRENCH, Yvonne. *Mrs. Gaskell*. London: Home & Van Thal, 1949. (Good brief survey of life and works.)

994 GANZ, Margaret. *Elizabeth Gaskell: The Artist in Conflict*. New York: Twayne, 1969.

995 HALDANE, Elizabeth. *Mrs. Gaskell and Her Friends*. London: Hodder & Stoughton, 1931.

996 HOPKINS, Annette B. "Dickens and Mrs. Gaskell." *HLQ*, 9(1946):357–85.

997 HOPKINS, Annette B. *Elizabeth Gaskell: Her Life and Work*. London: Lehmann, 1952.*

998 LEWIS, Naomi. *A Visit to Mrs. Wilcox*. London: Cresset, 1957.

999 LUCAS, John. "Mrs. Gaskell and Brotherhood." *Tradition and Tolerance in Nineteenth-Century Fiction: Critical Essays on Some English and American Novels*. Ed. David B. Howard, John Lucas, and John Goode. London: Routledge & Kegan Paul, 1966, pp. 141–205.

1000 PAYNE, George A. *Mrs. Gaskell: A Brief Biography*. Manchester, Eng.: Sherratt & Hughes, 1929.

1001 POLLARD, Arthur. *Mrs. Gaskell: Novelist and Biographer*. Manchester, Eng.: Manchester U P, 1965.*

1002 SANDERS, Gerald DeWitt. *Elizabeth Gaskell*. CSE 15. New Haven: Yale U P, 1929.

1003 VAN DULLEMEN, Johanna Jacoba. *Mrs. Gaskell, Novelist and Biographer*. Amsterdam: Paris, 1924.

1004 WHITFIELD, A. Stanton. *Mrs. Gaskell: Her Life and Work*. London: Routledge, 1929.

CRITICAL

See 52,* 88,* 170.

1005 COLLINS, H. P. "The Naked Sensibility: Elizabeth Gaskell." *EIC*, 3(1953):60–72.

1006 KETTLE, Arnold. "The Early Victorian Social-Problem Novel." In 45, pp. 169–87.*

1007 POLLARD, Arthur. "The Novels of Mrs. Gaskell." *BJRL*, 43(1961):403–25.

1008 QUILLER-COUCH, Arthur. *Charles Dickens and Other Victorians*. Cambridge: Cambridge U P, 1925.

1009 RUBENIUS, Aina. *The Woman Question in Mrs. Gaskell's Life and Works*. Cambridge, Mass.: Harvard U P, 1950.

1010 WILLIAMS, Raymond. "The Industrial Novels." See 136.

1011 WRIGHT, Edgar. *Mrs. Gaskell: The Basis for Reassessment*. London: Oxford U P, 1965.

CRANFORD

1012 DODSWORTH, Martin. "Women without Men at Cranford." *EIC*, 13(1963):132–45.

1013 SHORT, Clarice. "Studies in Gentleness." *WHR*, 11(1957):387–93. (Mrs. Gaskell's *Cranford* and Sarah Orne Jewett's *Country of the Pointed Firs*.)

1014 TARRATT, Margaret. "*Cranford* and 'the Strict Code of Gentility.'" *EIC*, 18(1968):152–63.

1015 WRIGHT, Edgar. "Mrs. Gaskell and the World of *Cranford*." *REL*, 6(1965):68–79.

MARY BARTON

See 96.*

1016 ALTICK, Richard D. "Dion Boucicault Stages *Mary Barton*." *NCF*, 14(1959):129–41.

1017 BLAND, D. S. "*Mary Barton* and Historical Accuracy." *RES*, n.s.1(1950):58–60.

1018 HOPKINS, Annette B. "*Mary Barton:* A Victorian Best Seller." *NCF*, 3(1948):1–18.

NORTH AND SOUTH

1019 BOWEN, Elizabeth. Introduction to *North and South*. London: Lehmann, 1951.

1020 CHAPPLE, J. A. "*North and South:* A Reassessment." *EIC*, 17(1967):461–72.

1021 SHORTER, Clement. Introduction to *North and South*. WC. London: Frowde, 1909.

Gleig, George Robert (1796–1888)

MAIN NOVELS

1022 *The Subaltern*, 1836. *The Chelsea Pensioners*. 3 vols., 1829. *Allan Breck. A Novel*. 3 vols., 1834. *The Hussar*. 2 vols., 1837.

Gore, Mrs. Catherine Grace Francis, née Moody (1799–1861)

MAIN NOVELS

1023 *Women as They Are, or The Manners of the Day.* 3 vols., 1830. *Mothers and Daughters. A Tale of the Year 1830.* 3 vols., 1831. *Cecil. Adventures of a Coxcomb.* 3 vols., 1841. *Cecil a Peer. A Sequel to Cecil; or, the Adventures of a Coxcomb.* 3 vols., 1841.

STUDIES

See 204.

Griffin, Gerald (1803–1840)

MAIN NOVELS

1024 *Tales of the Munster Festivals.* 3 vols., 1827. *The Collegians, or the Colleen Bawn. A Tale of Garryowen.* 3 vols., 1829. *The Rivals and Tracy's Ambition.* 3 vols., 1830.

STUDIES

See 188.

1025 FLANAGAN, Thomas B. "Gerald Griffin." See 38, pp. 205–51.*

1026 GRIFFIN, Daniel. *The Life of Gerald Griffin, Esq.* London, 1843.

1027 MANNIN, Ethel. *Two Studies in Integrity: Gerald Griffin and the Rev. Francis Mahoney ("Father Prout").* New York: Putnam, 1954.

Hannay, James (1827–1873)

MAIN NOVELS

1028 *Biscuits and Grog. Personal Reminiscences and Sketches by Percival Plug, R. N.,* 1848. *King Dobbs. Sketches in Ultra-Marine,* 1849. *Singleton Fontenoy, R. N.* 3 vols., 1850. *Eustace Conyers. A Novel.* 3 vols., 1855.

STUDIES

1029 WORTH, George J. *James Hannay: His Life and Works.* Lawrence: U of Kansas P, 1964.

Hardy, Thomas (1840–1928)

NOVELS

1030 *Desperate Remedies. A Novel.* 3 vols. London: Tinsley, 1871. *Under the Greenwood Tree. A Rural Painting of the Dutch School.* 2 vols. London: Tinsley, 1872. *A Pair of Blue Eyes. A Novel.* 3 vols. London: Tinsley, 1873. [First pub. in *Tinsley's Mag.*, 11, 12:1872–1873.] *Far from the Madding Crowd.* 2 vols. London: Smith, Elder, 1874. [First pub. anonymously in *Cornhill Mag.*, 29, 30:1874.] *The Hand of Ethelberta. A Comedy in Chapters.* 2 vols. London: Smith, Elder, 1876. [First pub. in *Cornhill Mag.*, 32, 33:1875–1876.] *The Return of the Native.* 3 vols. London: Smith, Elder, 1878. [First pub. in *Belgravia*, 34–37:1878.] *The Trumpet-Major. A Tale.* 3 vols. London: Smith, Elder, 1880. [First pub. in *Good Words*, Jan.–Dec., 1880.] *A Laodicean: or The Castle of the DeStancys. A Story of To-day.* 3 vols. London: Low, 1881. [First pub. in *Harper's Mag.* (European edition), 1–3:1880.] *The Romantic Adventures of a Milkmaid: A Novel.* New York: Harper, 1883. [First pub. in *The Graphic*, Summer, 1883.] *Two on a Tower: A Romance.* 3 vols. London: Low, 1882. [First pub. in *Atlantic Monthly*, 49, 50:1882.] *The Mayor of Casterbridge: The Life and Death of a Man of Character.* 2 vols. London: Smith, Elder, 1886. [First pub. in *The Graphic*, Jan. 2–May 15, 1886.] *The Woodlanders.* 3 vols. London: Macmillan, 1887. [First pub. in *Macmillan's Mag.*, 54, 55:1886–1887.] *Tess of the D'Urbervilles. A Pure Woman Faithfully Presented.* 3 vols. London: Osgood, McIlvaine, 1891. [Main portion first pub. in *The Graphic*, July 4–Dec. 26, 1891.] *Jude the Obscure.* London: Osgood, McIlvaine, 1895. [First pub. in abridged form in *Harper's Mag.*, 29, 30:1894–1895.] *The Well-Beloved. A Sketch of a Temperament.* London: Osgood, McIlvaine, 1897. [First pub. in *Illustrated London News*, Oct. 1–Dec. 17, 1892, as *The Pursuit of the Well-Beloved.*] *An Indiscretion in the Life of an Heiress.* London: [Privately printed], 1934. [First printed in *New Quarterly Mag.*, July, 1878.]

BIBLIOGRAPHY AND REFERENCE

See 25.*

1031 BEEBE, Maurice, Bonnie CULOTTA, and Erin MARCUS. "Criticism of Thomas Hardy: A Selected Checklist." *MFS*, 6(1960):258–79.*

1032 PURDY, Richard L. *Thomas Hardy: A Bibliographical Study.* London: Oxford U P, 1954.*

1033 WEBER, Carl J. *The First Hundred Years of Hardy, 1840–1940.* Waterville, Me.: Colby College Library, 1942.

TEXTS

1034 *Works.* Mellstock Edition. 37 vols. London: Macmillan, 1919–1920.

1035 *Works.* Wessex Edition. 23 vols. London: Macmillan, 1912–1931.

COLLECTIONS, LETTERS, ETC.

1036 HARDY, Evelyn, ed. *Thomas Hardy's Notebooks.* London: Hogarth, 1955.

1037 OREL, Harold, ed. *Thomas Hardy's Personal Writings. Prefaces, Literary Opinions, Reminiscences.* Lawrence: U of Kansas P, 1966.

1038 WEBER, Carl J., ed. *"Dearest Emmie": Thomas Hardy's Letters to His First Wife.* New York: St Martin's P, 1963.

1039 WEBER, Carl J., ed. *The Letters of Thomas Hardy.* Waterville, Me.: Colby College P, 1954. (Letters in Colby College collection only.)

BIOGRAPHICAL AND GENERAL

See 88.*

1040 HARDY, Evelyn. *Thomas Hardy: A Critical Biography.* London: Hogarth, 1954.*

1041 HARDY, Florence Emily. *The Life of Thomas Hardy, 1840-1928.* London: Macmillan, 1962. [Originally publ. as two vols.: *The Early Life of Thomas Hardy, 1840-1891.* New York: Macmillan, 1928; and *The Later Years of Thomas Hardy, 1892-1928.* New York: Macmillan, 1930.]*

1042 HAWKINS, Desmond. *Hardy the Novelist* [1951]. New York: Taplinger, 1966.

1043 LERNER, Laurence, and John HOLMSTROM, eds. *Thomas Hardy and His Readers: A Selection of Contemporary Reviews.* New York: Barnes & Noble, 1968.

1044 PINION, F. B. *A Hardy Companion: A Guide to the Works of Thomas Hardy and Their Background.* New York: St Martin's P, 1968.

1045 SAXELBY, F. O. *A Thomas Hardy Dictionary: The Characters and Scenes of the Novels and Poems Alphabetically Arranged and Described.* London: Routledge, 1911.

1046 WEBER, Carl J. *Hardy of Wessex: His Life and Literary Career* [1940]. Rev. ed. New York: Columbia U P, 1965.*

CRITICISM

See 6.*

1047 GUERARD, Albert J., ed. *Hardy: A Collection of Critical Essays.* TCV. Englewood Cliffs, N.J.: Prentice-Hall, 1963.*†

1048 ABERCROMBIE, Lascelles. *Thomas Hardy: A Critical Study.* London: Secker, 1912. Abridged version. New York: Viking, 1927.

1049 ANDERSEN, Carol Reed. "Time, Space and Perspective in Thomas Hardy." *NCF*, 9(1954):192-208.

1050 BAILEY, J. O. "Hardy's 'Mephistophelian Visitants.'" *PMLA*, 61(1946):1146-84.

1051 BEACH, Joseph Warren. *The Technique of Thomas Hardy.* Chicago: U of Chicago P, 1922.

1052 BROWN, Douglas. *Thomas Hardy.* WTW. London: Longmans, Green, 1954. Rev. ed. 1961. (Critical introduction.)

1053 CARPENTER, Richard C. "Hardy's 'Gargoyles.'" *MFS*, 6(1960):223-32.

1054 CECIL, Lord David. *Hardy the Novelist: An Essay in Criticism.* London: Constable, 1943.

1055 CHAPMAN, Frank. "Hardy the Novelist." *Scrutiny,* 3(1934):22-37.

1056 CHASE, Mary Ellen. *Thomas Hardy from Serial to Novel.* Minneapolis: U of Minnesota P, 1927.

1057 CHEW, Samuel C. *Thomas Hardy, Poet and Novelist.* New York: Knopf, 1928.

1058 DAVIDSON, Donald. "The Traditional Basis of Thomas Hardy's Fiction." *SoR,* 6(1940):162-78.

1059 DE LAURA, David J. " 'The Ache of Modernism' in Hardy's Later Novels." *ELH,* 34(1967):380-99.

1060 ELIOT, T. S. In *After Strange Gods.* London: Faber, 1934. (Hostile view of Hardy as a "modern heretic.")

1061 FIROR, Ruth A. *Folkways in Thomas Hardy.* Philadelphia: U of Pennsylvania P, 1931.†

1062 GOODHEART, Eugene. "Thomas Hardy and the Lyrical Novel." *NCF,* 12(1957):215-25.

1063 GUERARD, Albert J. *Thomas Hardy: The Novels and Stories.* Cambridge, Mass.: Harvard U P, 1949. Rev. ed. 1964.*†

1064 HOLLOWAY, John. *The Victorian Sage: Studies in Argument.* London: Macmillan, 1953, pp. 244-89.†

1065 HOWE, Irving. *Thomas Hardy.* Masters of World Literature. New York: Macmillan, 1967.*†

1066 HYDE, William J. "Hardy's View of Realism: A Key to the Rustic Characters." *VS,* 2(1958):45-59.

1067 JOHNSON, Lionel. *The Art of Thomas Hardy* [1894]. Rev. ed. New York: Dodd, Mead, 1923.

1068 LAWRENCE, D. H. "Study of Thomas Hardy." *Phoenix: The Posthumous Papers of D. H. Lawrence.* Ed. Edward D. McDonald. New York: Viking, 1936, pp. 398-516. (Originally a separate monograph; mainly illuminating about Lawrence.)*

1069 MC DOWALL, Arthur. *Thomas Hardy: A Critical Study.* London: Faber, 1931.

1070 MULLER, Herbert J. "The Novels of Hardy Today." *SoR,* (1940):214-24.

1071 MURRY, J. Middleton. *Wrap Me Up in My Aubusson Carpet.* New York: Greenberg, 1924. (Angry reply to George Moore's attack on Hardy in *Conversations in Ebury Street.* London, 1924.)

1072 PORTER, Katherine Anne. "Notes on a Criticism of Thomas Hardy." *SoR,* 6(1940):150-61. Repr. in her *The Days Before.* New York: Harcourt, Brace, 1952.

1073 RUTLAND, William R. *Thomas Hardy: A Study of His Writings and Their Background.* Oxford: Blackwell, 1938.*

1074 SCOTT, James F. "Thomas Hardy's Use of the Gothic: An Examination of Five Representative Works." *NCF*, 17(1963):363-80.

1075 STEWART, J. I. M. "Hardy." *Eight Modern Writers*. Oxford: Oxford U P, 1963, pp. 19-70.

1076 WEBSTER, Harvey C. *On a Darkling Plain: The Art and Thought of Thomas Hardy*. Chicago: U of Chicago P, 1947.

1077 WOOLF, Virginia. "Half of Thomas Hardy." *The Captain's Death Bed and Other Essays*. London: Hogarth, 1950, pp. 61-6. (Review of *The Early Life of Thomas Hardy*, by Florence Emily Hardy.)

1078 WOOLF, Virginia. "The Novels of Thomas Hardy." *The Second Common Reader*. New York: Harcourt Brace, 1932, pp. 266-80.†

1079 ZABEL, Morton Dauwen. "Hardy in Defense of His Art. The Aesthetic of Incongruity." *SoR*, 6(1940):125-49. Rev. and repr. in his *Craft and Character in Modern Fiction*. New York: Viking, 1957, pp. 70-96.

FAR FROM THE MADDING CROWD

See 64.*

1080 CARPENTER, Richard C. "The Mirror and the Sword: Imagery in *Far from the Madding Crowd*." *NCF*, 18(1964):331-45.

1081 PURDY, Richard L. Introduction to *Far from the Madding Crowd*. Boston: Houghton Mifflin, 1957.†

1082 WEBER, Carl J. Introduction to *Far from the Madding Crowd*. New York: Holt, Rinehart, 1959.†

JUDE THE OBSCURE

See 48, 64,* 1047, 1068.*

1083 CLIFFORD, Emma. "The Child: The Circus: and *Jude the Obscure*." *Cambridge Journal*, 7(1954):531-46.

1084 GREGOR, Ian. "*Jude the Obscure*." In 913, 237-56.

1085 HEILMAN, Robert B. "Hardy's Sue Bridehead." *NCF*, 20(1966):307-23.*

1086 HOLLAND, Norman. "*Jude the Obscure*: Hardy's Symbolic Indictment of Christianity." *NCF*, 9(1954):50-60.

1087 HOOPES, Kathleen R. "Illusion and Reality in *Jude the Obscure*." *NCF*, 12(1957):154-7.

1088 HOWE, Irving. Introduction to *Jude the Obscure*. Boston: Houghton Mifflin, 1965.†

1089 LAWYER, W. R. "Thomas Hardy's *Jude the Obscure*." *Punch*, 28(1967):6-54.

1090 MC DOWELL, Frederick P. W. "Hardy's 'Seemings or Personal Impressions': The Symbolic Use of Image and Contrast in *Jude the Obscure*." *MFS*, 6(1960):233-50.

1091 MIZENER, Arthur. "*Jude the Obscure* as a Tragedy." *SoR*, 6(1940):193-213.

1092 MIZENER, Arthur. "The Novel of Doctrine in the Nineteenth Century: Hardy's *Jude the Obscure.*" *The Sense of Life in the Modern Novel.* Boston: Houghton Mifflin, 1964, pp. 55-78.†

1093 SLACK, Robert C. "The Text of Hardy's *Jude the Obscure.*" *NCF*, 11(1957):251-75.

THE MAYOR OF CASTERBRIDGE

1094 DAVIDSON, Donald. "Futurism and Archaism in Toynbee and Hardy." *Still Rebels, Still Yankees, and Other Essays.* Baton Rouge: Louisiana State U P, 1957, pp. 62-83.

1095 DIKE, D. A. "A Modern Oedipus: *The Mayor of Casterbridge.*" *EIC*, 2(1952):169-79.

1096 FRIEDMAN, Norman. "Criticism and the Novel." *AR*, 18(1958):348-52.

1097 GARDNER, W. H. *Some Thoughts on* The Mayor of Casterbridge. English Associations Pamphlets 77. Oxford: Oxford U P, 1930.

1098 HEILMAN, Robert B. "Hardy's *Mayor:* Notes on Style." *NCF*, 18(1964):307-29.

1099 KARL, Frederick R. "*The Mayor of Casterbridge:* A New Fiction Defined." *MFS*, 6(1960):195-213.

1100 KIELY, Robert. "Vision and Viewpoint in *The Mayor of Casterbridge.*" *NCF*, 23(1968):189-200.

1101 MOYNAHAN, Julian. "*The Mayor of Casterbridge* and the Old Testament First Book of Samuel: A Study of Some Literary Relationships." *PMLA*, 71(1956):118-30.

1102 PATERSON, John. "*The Mayor of Casterbridge* as Tragedy." *VS*, 3(1959):151-72. Also in 1047, pp. 91-112.*

1103 SCHWEIK, Robert C. "Character and Fate in Hardy's *The Mayor of Casterbridge.*" *NCF*, 21(1966):249-62.

THE RETURN OF THE NATIVE

1104 DEAN, Leonard W. "Heroism and Pathos in Hardy's *Return of the Native.*" *NCF*, 15(1960):207-20.

1105 EMERY, John P. "Chronology in Hardy's *Return of the Native.*" *PMLA*, 54(1939):618-20.

1106 GOLDBERG, M. A. "Hardy's Double-Visioned Universe." *EIC*, 7(1957):374-82.

1107 HAGAN, John. "A Note on the Significance of Diggory Venn." *NCF*, 16(1961):147-56.

1108 PATERSON, John. *The Making of* The Return of the Native. Berkeley: U of California P, 1960.*

1109 PATERSON, John. "The 'Poetics' of *The Return of the Native.*" *MFS*, 6(1960):214-22.

1110 PATERSON, John. "*The Return of the Native* as Antichristian Document." *NCF*, 14(1959):111-27.

1111 SCHWEIK, R. C. "Theme, Character, and Perspective in Hardy's *The Return of the Native.*" *PQ*, 41(1962):757-67.

1112 WALCUTT, Charles C. "Character and Coincidence in *The Return of the Native.*" In 93, pp. 153-73.

TESS OF THE D'URBERVILLES

See 64,* 71,* 98,* 191.

1113 ELLEDGE, Scott, ed. *Tess of the D'Urbervilles: An Authoritative Text, Hardy and the Novel, Criticism.* New York: Norton, 1965.†

1114 LA VALLEY, Albert J., ed. *"Tess of the d'Urbervilles": A Collection of Critical Essays.* TCL. Englewood Cliffs, N.J.: Prentice-Hall, 1969.†

1115 BRICK, Allan. "Paradise and Consciousness in Hardy's *Tess.*" *NCF*, 17(1962):115-34.

1116 BUCKLER, William E. Introduction to *Tess of the D'Urbervilles.* Boston: Houghton Mifflin, 1960.†

1117 GREGOR, Ian, and Brian NICHOLAS. "The Novel as Moral Protest: *Tess of the D'Urbervilles.*" In 913, pp. 123-50.*

1118 LODGE, David. "Tess, Nature, and the Voices of Hardy." In 74, pp. 164-88.

1119 PARIS, Bernard J. "'A Confusion of Many Standards.'" *NCF*, 24(1969):57-79.

1120 TANNER, Tony. "Colour and Movement in Hardy's *Tess of the d'Urbervilles.*" *CritQ*, 10(1968):219-39.*

THE WOODLANDERS

1121 DRAKE, Robert Y., Jr. "*The Woodlanders* as Traditional Pastoral." *MFS*, 6(1960):251-7.

1122 FAYEN, George. "*The Woodlanders:* Inwardness and Memory." *SEL*, 1(1961):81-100.

1123 MATCHETT, William H. "*The Woodlanders*, or Realism in Sheep's Clothing." *NCF*, 9(1955):241-61.

UNDER THE GREENWOOD TREE

1124 DANBY, John F. "Under the Greenwood Tree." *CritQ*, 1(1959):5-13.

1125 TOLIVER, Harold E. "The Dance under the Greenwood Tree: Hardy's Bucolics." *NCF*, 17(1962):57-68.

Hogg, James (1770-1835)

MAIN NOVELS

1126 *The Private Memoirs and Confessions of a Justified Sinner* [Anon.]. 1824.

STUDIES

See Craig, 173.*

1127 BATHO, E. C. *The Ettrick Shepherd*. Cambridge, Eng.: Cambridge U P, 1927. (Includes bibliography.)

1128 GIDE, André. Introduction to *Private Memoirs and Confessions of a Justified Sinner*. London: Cresset, 1947.

1129 SIMPSON, Louis. *James Hogg: A Critical Study*. Edinburgh: Oliver & Boyd, 1962.

Hook, Theodore Edward (1788-1841)

MAIN NOVELS

1130 *Maxwell*. 3 vols., 1830. *The Parson's Daughter*. 3 vols., 1833. *Gilbert Gurney*. 3 vols., 1836. *Jack Brag*. 3 vols., 1837. *Fathers and Sons: A Novel*. 3 vols., 1842. *Peregrine Bunce; or, Settled at Last*. 3 vols., 1842.

STUDIES

1131 BRIGHTFIELD, Myron T. *Theodore Hook and His Novels*. Cambridge, Mass.: Harvard U P, 1928.

1132 REPPLIER, Agnes. In *Pursuit of Laughter*. New York: Houghton Mifflin, 1936, pp. 111-24. (Anecdotal treatment as a figure in the history of humor.)

Hughes, Thomas (1822-1896)

MAIN NOVELS

1133 *Tom Brown's School Days. By an Old Boy*, 1857. *Tom Brown at Oxford*. 3 vols., 1861.

STUDIES

1134 MACK, E. C. and W. H. G. ARMYTAGE. *Thomas Hughes: The Life of the Author of* Tom Brown's School Days. London: Benn, 1952.

James, George Payne Rainsford (1799-1860)

MAIN NOVELS

1135 *Richelieu. A Tale of France*. 3 vols., 1829. *Darnley, or The Field of the Cloth of Gold*. 3 vols., 1830. *De L'Orme*. 3 vols., 1830. *Philip Augustus, or The Brothers in Arms*. 3 vols., 1831. *Henry Masterton, or The Adventures of a Young Cavalier*. 3 vols., 1832. *Mary of Burgundy, or The Revolt of Ghent*. 3 vols., 1833. *The Huguenot. A Tale of the French Protestants*. 3 vols., 1839.

STUDIES

1136 ELLIS, S. M. *The Solitary Horseman.* Kensington: Cayme, 1927.

Jefferies, Richard (1848–1887)

MAIN NOVELS

1137 *Wood Magic. A Fable.* 2 vols., 1881. *Bevis: The Story of a Boy.* 3 vols., 1882. *The Dewy Morn.* 2 vols., 1884.

EDITIONS AND STUDIES

1138 ELWIN, Malcolm, ed. *The Essential Jefferies.* London: Cape, 1948.

1139 JEFFERIES, Richard. *The Story of My Heart. My Autobiography.* London: Duckworth, 1912. [First pub. in 1883.]

1140 KEITH, W. J. *Richard Jefferies: A Critical Study.* Toronto: U of Toronto P, 1965.

1141 LEAVIS, Q. D. "Lives and Works of Richard Jefferies." *Scrutiny,* 6(1938):435–46.

1142 LOOKER, Samuel J., and Crichton PORTEOUS. *Richard Jefferies, Man of the Fields: A Biography and Letters.* London: Baker, 1965.

1143 WARREN, C. Henry, ed. *Collected Works of Richard Jefferies.* London: Eyre & Spottiswoode, 1948.

1144 WILLIAMSON, Henry. "Some Nature Writers and Civilization." *EDH,* 30(1960):1–18.

Jewsbury, Geraldine Endsor (1812–1880)

MAIN NOVELS

1145 *Zoe: the History of Two Lives.* 3 vols., 1845. *Marian Withers.* 3 vols., 1851. *The Sorrows of Gentility.* 2 vols., 1856.

STUDIES

1146 HOWE, Susanne. *Geraldine Jewsbury: Her Life and Errors.* London: Allen & Unwin, 1935.

1147 IRELAND, Mrs. A., ed. *A Selection from the Letters of Geraldine Jewsbury to Jane Welsh Carlyle.* London and New York: Longmans, Green, 1892.

1148 WOOLF, Virginia. "Geraldine and Jane." In 1078, pp. 186–201. ("Geraldine" is Geraldine Jewsbury; "Jane" is Mrs. Carlyle.)†

Kingsley, Charles (1819-1875)

NOVELS

1149 *Alton Locke, Tailor and Poet.* 2 vols. London: Chapman & Hall, 1850. *Yeast, a Problem.* [*Fraser's Mag.*, July-Dec. 1848.] London: Chapman & Hall, 1851. *Hypatia, or New Foes with an Old Face.* [*Fraser's Mag.*, Jan. 1852-April 1853.] 2 vols. London: Parker, 1853. *Westward Ho! or the Voyages and Adventures of Sir Amyas Leigh, Knight, of Burrough, in the County of Devon, in the Reign of Her Most Glorious Majesty Queen Elizabeth.* 3 vols. Cambridge: Macmillan, 1855. *Two Years Ago.* 3 vols. Cambridge: Macmillan, 1857.

1150 *Hereward the Wake, "Last of the English."* [*Good Words*, Jan.-Dec. 1865.] 2 vols. London and Cambridge: Macmillan, 1866.

BIBLIOGRAPHY

See 25,* 1153, 1156, 1164.*

1151 PARRISH, Morris L. *Charles Kingsley and Thomas Hughes.* London: Constable, 1936.

COLLECTED EDITIONS, LETTERS

1152 *The Novels, Poems, and Letters of Charles Kingsley.* Including memoir by Thomas Hughes. 14 vols. New York, London: Co-Operative Publication Society, 1898-1899.

1153 *The Works of Charles Kingsley.* 28 vols. London: Macmillan, 1880-1885. (Most complete.)

1154 KINGSLEY, Frances E. *Charles Kingsley: His Letters and Memories of His Life.* London: Paul, 1878.

1155 MARTIN, Robert B. *Charles Kingsley's American Notes.* Princeton: Princeton U Library, 1958.

BIOGRAPHICAL AND GENERAL

1156 BALDWIN, Stanley E. *Charles Kingsley.* Ithaca: Cornell U P, 1934. (Includes extensive bibliography about Kingsley and his works.)

1157 BROWN, William Henry. *Charles Kingsley: The Work and Influence of Parson Lot.* Manchester, Eng.: Co-Operative Union, 1924.

1158 FORD, George H. "The Governor Eyre Case in England." *UTQ*, 17(1948):219-33.

1159 HANAWALT, Mary W. "Charles Kingsley and Science." *SP*, 34(1937):589-611.

1160 KENDALL, Guy. *Charles Kingsley and His Ideas.* London and New York: Hutchinson, 1947.

1161 MARRIOTT, J. A. R. *Charles Kingsley: Novelist.* London, 1892.

1162 MARTIN, Robert B. *The Dust of Combat: A Life of Charles Kingsley.* New York: Norton, 1959.*

1163 POPE-HENNESSY, Una. *Canon Charles Kingsley.* London: Chatto & Windus, 1948.

1164 THORP, Margaret F. *Charles Kingsley: 1819-1875.* Princeton: Princeton U P, 1937.*

1165 VULLIAMY, Colwyn E. *Charles Kingsley and Christian Socialism.* London: Fabian Society, 1914.

CRITICAL

See 136, 170.

1166 BEER, Gillian. "Charles Kingsley and the Literary Image of the Countryside." *VS,* 8(1965):243-54.

1167 BLINDERMAN, Charles S. "Huxley and Kingsley." *VN,* 20(1961):25-8.

1168 CONACHER, W. M. "Charles Kingsley." *QQ,* 45(1938):503-11.

1169 JOHNSTON, Arthur. "*The Water Babies:* Kingsley's Debt to Darwin." *English,* 12(1959):215-19.

1170 KETTLE, Arnold. "The Early Victorian Social-Problem Novel." In 39, pp. 169-87.*

1171 LODGE, David. Introduction to *Alton Locke: Tailor and Poet.* London: Cassell, 1967.

1172 LORD, W. F. "The Kingsley Novels." *Nineteenth Century,* 55(1904):996-1004.

1173 NICOL, Albert. *Charles Kingsley und die Geschichte.* Munich, 1936.

1174 PRICE, J. B. "Charles Reade and Charles Kingsley." *ContempR,* 183(1953):161-6.

1175 WELTE, Hilda. *Das heroische Element bei Charles Kingsley.* Freiburg im Breisgau, 1934. (Doctoral dissertation.)

Kingsley, Henry (1830-1876)

MAIN NOVELS

1176 *Ravenshoe.* 3 vols., 1861. *The Recollections of Geoffrey Hamlyn.* 3 vols., 1859. *Austin Elliott.* 2 vols., 1863. *The Hillyars and the Burtons: A Story of Two Families.* 3 vols., 1865. *Mademoiselle Mathilde.* 3 vols., 1868.

STUDIES

See 1754.*

1177 ELLIS, S. M. *Henry Kingsley, 1830-1876. Towards a Vindication.* London: Richards, 1931.

1178 SADLEIR, Michael. "Henry Kingsley: A Portrait." *Edinburgh R,* 240(1924):330-48.

1179 THIRKELL, Angela. "Henry Kingsley, 1830–1876." *NCF*, 5(1950):175–87.

1180 THIRKELL, Angela. "The Works of Henry Kingsley." *NCF*, 5(1951):273–93.

1181 WOLFF, R. L. "Henry Kingsley." *Harvard Library Bull*, 13(1959):195–226.

Lawrence, George Alfred (1827–1876)

MAIN NOVEL

1182 *Guy Livingstone; or, "Thorough,"* 1857.

STUDY

1183 FLEMING, G. H. *George Alfred Lawrence and the Victorian Sensation Novel.* U of Arizona Bull. 33. Tucson: U of Arizona P, 1952.

Le Fanu, Joseph Sheridan (1814–1873)

MAIN NOVELS

1184 *The Cock and the Anchor: Being a Chronicle of Old Dublin City.* 3 vols., 1845. *The House by the Church-Yard.* 3 vols., 1863. *Wylder's Hand. A Novel.* 3 vols., 1864. *Uncle Silas. A Tale of Bartram-Haugh.* 3 vols., 1864. *Guy Deverell.* 3 vols., 1865. *The Wyvern Mystery. A Novel.* 3 vols., 1868.

STUDIES

1185 BROWNE, Nelson. *Sheridan Le Fanu.* London: Barker, 1951.

1186 ELLIS, S. M. *Wilkie Collins, Le Fanu and Others.* London: Constable, 1931.

1187 PRITCHETT, V. S. "An Irish Ghost." See 87.*

1188 SHROYER, Frederick. Introduction to *Uncle Silas.* New York: Dover, 1966. (This, and much else of Le Fanu's, is available in paperback eds.)

Lever, Charles James (1806–1872)

MAIN NOVELS

1189 *The Confessions of Harry Lorrequer,* 1839. *Charles O'Malley, the Irish Dragoon.* 2 vols., 1841. *Jack Hinton,* 1843. [Originally pub. with *Tom Burke* as part of *Our Mess.*]

1190 *Tom Burke of "Ours,"* 1844. [Originally pub. as part of *Our Mess.*] *The Knight of Gwynne: A Tale of the Time of the Union,* 1847. *Davenport Dunn; or, the Man of the Day,* 1859. *A Day's Ride.* 2 vols., 1863.

STUDIES

1191 *The Novels of Charles Lever.* Ed. by his daughter [Julia Kate Neville]. 37 vols. London: Downey, 1897–1899.

1192 DOWNEY, Edmund. *Charles Lever: His Life in His Letters.* New York: Scribner's, 1906.

1193 FITZPATRICK, W. J. *Life of Charles Lever.* 2 vols. London: Chapman & Hall, 1879.

1194 STEVENSON, Lionel. *Doctor Quicksilver: The Life of Charles Lever.* London: Chapman & Hall, 1939.*

Linton, Eliza Lynn, née Lynn (1822–1898)

MAIN NOVELS

1195 *Lizzie Norton of Greyrigg.* 3 vols., 1866. *The True History of Joshua Davidson,* 1872. *Patricia Kemball.* 3 vols., 1874. *The Atonement of Leam Dundas.* 3 vols., 1877. *The Autobiography of Christopher Kirkland.* 3 vols., 1885.

STUDIES

1196 LAYARD, G. S. *Eliza Lynn Linton: Her Life, Letters and Opinions.* London: Methuen, 1901.

1197 LINTON, Eliza Lynn. *My Literary Life.* London, 1899.

Lover, Samuel (1797–1868)

MAIN NOVELS

1198 *Rory O'More. A National Romance.* 3 vols., 1837. *Handy Andy. A Tale of Irish Life,* 1842.

STUDIES

See 80.

1199 BERNARD, W. B. *The Life of Samuel Lover, Artistic, Literary and Musical.* 2 vols. London: King, 1874.

MacDonald, George (1824–1905)

MAIN NOVELS

1200 *Phantastes: A Faery Romance for Men and Women,* 1858. *David Elginbrod.* 3 vols., 1863. *Alec Forbes of Howglen.* 3 vols., 1865. *Annals of a Quiet Neighborhood.* 3 vols., 1867. [First pub. anonymously in *Sunday Mag.,* 1866.] *Robert Falconer.* 3 vols., 1868. [First pub. in *The Argosy,* 1867.] *At the Back of the North Wind,* 1871. [First pub. in *Good Words for the Young.*] *Malcolm.* 3 vols., 1875. *Sir Gibbie.* 3 vols., 1879. *Lilith: A Romance,* 1895.

STUDIES

1201 *George MacDonald: An Anthology.* Ed. C. S. Lewis. London: Bles, 1946.

1202 *Phantastes and Lilith.* Introduction by C. S. Lewis. Grand Rapids: Erdmans, 1964.†

1203 *The Visionary Novels of George MacDonald:* Lilith, Phantastes. Ed. Anne Fremantle. Introduction by W. H. Auden. New York: Noonday P, 1954.

1204 COLVILLE, K. N. *Fame's Twilight.* London: Allan, 1923.

1205 MAC DONALD, Greville. *George MacDonald and His Wife.* London: Allen & Unwin, 1924.

1206 TANNER, Tony. "Mountains and Depths—An Approach to Nineteenth-Century Dualism." *REL,* 3(1961):51-61.

1207 WOLFF, Robert Lee. *The Golden Keys: A Study of the Fiction of George MacDonald.* New Haven: Yale U P, 1961.

Mallock, William (1849-1923)

MAIN NOVELS

1208 *The New Republic, or Culture, Faith and Philosophy in an English Country House.* 2 vols., 1877. *The New Paul and Virginia, or Positivism on an Island,* 1878. *A Romance of the Nineteenth Century.* 2 vols., 1881.

STUDIES

1209 NICKERSON, Charles C. "A Bibliography of the Novels of W. H. Mallock." *ELT,* 6(1963):190-8.

1210 *The New Republic.* Ed. J. Max Patrick. Gainesville: U of Florida P, 1954. (Annotated; unevenly.)

1211 ADAMS, Amy B. *The Novels of William Hurrell Mallock.* U of Maine Studies, Second Series 34. Orono: U of Maine, 1934.

1212 TUCKER, Albert V. "W. H. Mallock and Late Victorian Conservatism." *UTQ,* 31(1962):223-41.

1213 YARKER, P. M. "Mallock's Other Novels." *NCF,* 14(1959):189-205.

Marryat, Frederick (1792–1848)

MAIN NOVELS

1214 *The Naval Officer; or, Scenes and Adventures in the Life of Frank Mildmay.* London: Colburn, 1829. *The King's Own.* London: Colburn & Bentley, 1830. *Newton Forster; or, the Merchant Service.* London: Cochrane, 1832. *Peter Simple.* [*Metropolitan Mag.*, June 1832–Dec. 1833.] London: Saunders & Otley, 1834. *Jacob Faithful.* [*Metropolitan Mag.*, Sept. 1833–Dec. 1834.] London: Saunders & Otley, 1834. *Japhet in Search of a Father.* [*Metropolitan Mag.*, Oct. 1834–Jan. 1836.] London: Saunders & Otley, 1836. *Mr. Midshipman Easy.* London: Saunders & Otley, 1836. *Snarleyow or, the Dog Fiend.* [*Metropolitan Mag.*, Feb. 1836–July 1837.] London: Colburn, 1837. *The Phantom Ship.* [*New Monthly Mag.*, 1837.] London: Colburn, 1839. *Masterman Ready; or, the Wreck of the Pacific.* London: Longman, 1841–1842.*The Children of the New Forest.* London: Hurst, 1847.

BIBLIOGRAPHY, COLLECTED WORKS, ETC.

See 22.

1215 *The Novels of Captain Marryat.* Ed. R. B. Johnson. 26 vols. London: Dent, 1929–1930.

BIOGRAPHICAL AND CRITICAL

1216 BOAS, F. S. "Captain Marryat." *QQ*, 44(1937):230–41.

1217 CONRAD, Joseph. "Tales of the Sea." (1898) *Notes on Life and Letters.* Garden City, N.Y., and Toronto: Doubleday, Page, 1921.

1218 DOUBLEDAY, Neal F. "Jack Easy and Billy Budd." *ELN*, 2(1964):39–42.

1219 HANNAY, David. *The Life of Frederick Marryat.* Robertson's Great Writers. London, 1889.

1220 LLOYD, Christopher. *Captain Marryat and the Old Navy.* London and New York: Longmans, Green, 1939.

1221 MARRYAT, Florence. *The Life and Letters of Captain Marryat.* 2 vols. London: Bentley, 1872.

1222 RICHMOND, H. W. "The Naval Officer in Fiction." *E&S*, 30(1944):7–25.

1223 SADLEIR, Michael. "Captain Marryat, A Portrait." *LMerc*, 10(1924):495–510.

1224 SCHUHMANN, Kuno. "Phrenologie und Ideologie: Frederick Marryats *Mr. Midshipman Easy.*" NS, 12(1964):567–73.

1225 WARNER, Oliver. *Captain Marryat, A Rediscovery.* London: Constable, 1953.

1226 WARNER, Oliver. "Mr. Golding and Marryat's *Little Savage.*" *REL*, 5(1964):51–5.

1227 WOOLF, Virginia. "The Captain's Death Bed." *The Captain's Death Bed and Other Essays*. London: Hogarth, 1950, pp. 39–48. (The Captain is Marryat.)

1228 ZANGER, Jules. "Marryat, Monsieur Violet, and Edward LaSalle." *NCF*, 12(1957):226–31.

Martineau, Harriet (1802–1876)

NOVELS

1229 *Deerbrook*. 3 vols., 1839. *The Hour and the Man: An Historical Romance*. 3 vols., 1841.

STUDIES

1230 BOSANQUET, Theodora. *Harriet Martineau*. London: Etschells & Macdonald, 1927.

1231 NEVILLE, J. C. *Harriet Martineau*. London: Muller, 1943.

1232 WEBB, R. K. *Harriet Martineau: A Radical Victorian*. London: Heinemann, 1960.

Meredith, George (1828–1909)

NOVELS

1233 *The Shaving of Shagpat: An Arabian Entertainment*. London: Chapman & Hall, 1855. *Farina: A Legend of Cologne*. London: Smith, Elder, 1857. *The Ordeal of Richard Feverel: A History of Father and Son*. 3 vols. London: Chapman & Hall, 1859. [Rev. by Meredith for an ed. pub. in 1878 by Kegan Paul.] *Evan Harrington; or, He would be a Gentleman*. New York: Harper, 1860. *Emilia in England*. 3 vols. London: Chapman & Hall, 1864. [Subsequently retitled *Sandra Belloni* (1866).] *Rhoda Fleming: A Story*. 3 vols. London: Tinsley, 1865. *Vittoria*. 3 vols. London: Chapman & Hall, 1867. *The Adventures of Harry Richmond*. 3 vols. London: Smith, Elder, 1871. *Beauchamp's Career*. 3 vols. London: Chapman & Hall, 1875. *The Egoist, a Comedy in Narrative*. 3 vols. London: Paul, 1879. *The Tragic Comedians: A Study in a Well-Known Story*. 2 vols. London: Chapman & Hall, 1880.

1234 *Diana of the Crossways: A Novel*. 3 vols. London: Chapman & Hall, 1885. *One of Our Conquerors*. 3 vols. London: Chapman & Hall, 1891. *Lord Ormont and His Aminta: A Novel*. 3 vols. London: Chapman & Hall, 1894. *The Amazing Marriage*. 2 vols. Westminster: Constable, 1895. *Celt and Saxon*. London: Constable, 1910. [Not completed.]

BIBLIOGRAPHY

See 25.*

1235 FORMAN, M. Buxton. *A Bibliography of the Writings in Prose and Verse of George Meredith*. London: Bibliographical Society, 1922.

1236 FORMAN, M. Buxton, ed. *Meredithiana*. London: Bibliographical Society, 1924.

1237 SAWIN, H. Lewis. "George Meredith: A Bibliography of Meredithiana, 1920-1953." *BB*, 21(1956):181-91, 215-6.

COLLECTIONS, LETTERS

1238 *Works*. "Memorial Edition." 29 vols. New York: Scribner's, 1909-1912. (No wholly satisfactory edition: this has the weaker revised version of *Richard Feverel*.)

1239 MEREDITH, W. M., ed. *Letters of George Meredith*. 2 vols. New York: Scribner's, 1912.

1240 *The Letters of George Meredith to Alice Meynell, with Annotations Thereto, 1896-1907*. London: Nonesuch, 1923.

1241 COOLIDGE, Bertha, ed. *A Catalogue of the Altschul Collection of George Meredith*. Boston: Private printing, 1931. (Contains additional letters.)

BIOGRAPHICAL AND GENERAL

1242 ABLE, Augustus Henry, III. *George Meredith and Thomas Love Peacock: A Study in Literary Influence*. Philadelphia: U of Pennsylvania P, 1933.

1243 GALLAND, René. *George Meredith, Les cinquante premières années: 1828-1878*. Paris: Les Presses Françaises, 1923.

1244 GRETTON, Mary Stuge. *The Writings and Life of George Meredith*. Cambridge, Mass.: Harvard U P, 1926.

1245 LINDSAY, Jack. *George Meredith: His Life and Work*. London: Bodley Head, 1956.

1246 PEEL, Robert. *The Creed of a Victorian Pagan*. Cambridge, Mass.: Harvard U P, 1931.

1247 SASSOON, Siegfried. *Meredith*. New York: Viking, 1948.

1248 STEVENSON, Lionel. *The Ordeal of George Meredith*. New York: Scribner's, 1953.*

CRITICAL

1249 AUSTIN, Deborah S. "Meredith on the Nature of Metaphor." *UTQ*, 27(1957):96-102.

1250 BARTLETT, Phyllis. "The Novels of George Meredith." *REL*, 3(1962):31-46.

1251 BARTLETT, Phyllis. "Richard Feverel, Knight-Errant." *BNYPL*, 63(1959):329-40.

1252 BEACH, Joseph Warren. *The Comic Spirit in George Meredith*. New York: Longmans, 1911, 1963.

1253 BEER, Gillian. "*The Amazing Marriage*: A Study in Contraries." *REL*, 7(1966):92-105.

1254 BEER, Gillian. "Meredith's Idea of Comedy: 1876-1880." *NCF*, 20(1965):165-76.

1255 BEER, Gillian. "Meredith's Revisions of *The Tragic Comedians*." *RES*, n.s.14(1963):33-53.

1256 BOOTH, Thornton Y. *Mastering the Event: Commitment to Fact in George Meredith's Fiction*. Utah State U Monograph, Ser. xiv, 2. Logan: Utah State P, 1967.

1257 BRUNNER, Bernard A. "Meredith's Symbolism: *Lord Ormont and His Aminta*." *NCF*, 8(1953):124-33.

1258 BUCHEN, Irving H. "The Egoists in *The Egoist:* The Sensualists and The Ascetics." *NCF*, 19(1964):255-69.

1259 BUCHEN, Irving H. "The Importance of the Minor Characters in *The Ordeal of Richard Feverel*." *BUSE*, 5(1961):154-66.

1260 CURTIN, Frank D. "Adrian Harley: The Limits of Meredith's Comedy." *NCF*, 7(1953):272-82.

1261 EAKER, J. Gordon. "Meredith's Human Comedy." *NCF*, 5(1951):253-72.

1262 FANGER, Donald. "George Meredith as Novelist." *NCF*, 16(1962):317-28.*

1263 FANGER, Donald. "Joyce and Meredith: A Question of Influence and Tradition." *MFS*, 6(1960):124-30.

1264 FRIEDMAN, Norman. "The Jangled Harp: Symbolic Structure in *Modern Love*." *MLQ*, 17(1957):9-26.

1265 GALLAND, René. *George Meredith and British Criticism: 1851-1909*. Paris: Les Presses Françaises, 1923.

1266 GETTMANN, Royal A. "Meredith as Publisher's Reader." *JEGP*, 48(1949):45-56.

1267 GETTMANN, Royal A. "Serialization and Evan Harrington." PMLA, 64(1949):963-75.

1268 GUDAS, Fabian. "George Meredith's *One of Our Conquerors*." In 88, pp. 222-33.*

1269 HARDY, Barbara. " 'A Way to your Hearts through Fire or Water': The Structure of Imagery in *Harry Richmond*." *EIC*, 10(1960):163-80.*

1270 HERGENHAN, L. T. "Meredith's Revisions of *Harry Richmond*." *RES*, n.s.14(1963):24-32.

1271 HILL, Charles J. "George Meredith's 'Plain Story.' " *NCF*, 7(1952):90-102. (*Rhoda Fleming*.)

1272 HILL, Charles J. "The Portrait of the Author in *Beauchamp's Career*." *JEGP*, 52(1953):332-9.

1273 HILL, Charles J. "Theme and Image in *The Egoist*." *UKCR*, 20(1954):281-5.

1274 HUDSON, Richard B. "The Meaning of Egoism in George Meredith's *The Egoist*." *NCF*, 3(1948):163-76.

1275 KARL, Frederick R. "*Beauchamp's Career:* An English Ordeal." *NCF*, 16(1961):117-31.

1276 KELVIN, Norman. *A Troubled Eden: Nature and Society in the Works of George Meredith.* Stanford: Stanford U P, 1961.

1277 KRUPPA, Joseph E. "Meredith's Late Novels: Suggestions for a Critical Approach." *NCF,* 19(1964):271-86.

1278 LANDIS, Joseph C. "George Meredith's Comedy." *BUSE,* 2(1956):17-35.

1279 LEES, F. N. "George Meredith: Novelist." In 39, Vol. VI, pp. 324-37.*

1280 LEWIS, C. Day. "George Meredith and Responsibility." *Notable Images of Virtue.* Toronto: Ryerson, 1954.

1281 LUBBOCK, Percy. In 75, ch. 9. (On *Harry Richmond.*)*

1282 MC KECHNIE, James. *Meredith's Allegory "The Shaving of Shagpat."* New York: Hodder & Stoughton, 1910.

1283 MORRIS, John W. "Inherent Principles of Order in *Richard Feverel." PMLA,* 78(1963):333-40.

1284 MUELLER, William R. "Theological Dualism and the 'System' in *Richard Feverel." ELH,* 18(1951):138-54.

1285 PETTER, Guy B. *George Meredith and His German Critics.* London: Witherby, 1939.

1286 POSTON, Lawrence, III. "Dramatic Reference and Structure in *The Ordeal of Richard Feverel." SEL,* 6(1967):743-52.

1287 PRIESTLEY, J. B. *George Meredith.* New York: Macmillan, 1926.

1288 STEVENSON, Lionel. "Meredith and the Problem of Style in the Novel." *Zeitschrift Für Anglistik and Americanistik* (East Berlin), 6(1958):181-9.

1289 STEVENSON, Lionel. "Meredith's Atypical Novel: A Study of *Rhoda Fleming." ES,* 11(1955):89-109.

1290 SUDRANN, Jean. " 'The Linked Eye and Mind': A Concept of Action in the Novels of Meredith." *SEL,* 4(1964):617-35.*

1291 TALON, Henri A. "Le Comique, le tragique, et le romanesque dans *The Ordeal of Richard Feverel." EA,* 17(1964):241-61.

1292 THOMAS, Sir William Beach. "George Meredith." In 79, vol. II, pp. 295-309.

1293 THOMSON, Fred C. "The Design of *One of Our Conquerors." SEL,* 2(1962):463-80.

1294 VAN GHENT, Dorothy. In 98, pp. 183-94. (On *The Egoist.*)*

1295 WATSON, Robert W. "George Meredith's *Sandra Belloni:* The 'Philosopher' on the Sentimentalists." *ELH,* 24(1957):321-35.

1296 WILLIAMS, I. M. "The Organic Structure of the *Ordeal of Richard Feverel." RES* 18(1967):16-29.

1297 WOOLF, Virginia. "On Rereading Meredith." *Granite and Rainbow Essays.* London: Hogarth, 1958, pp. 48-52.

1298 WOOLF, Virginia. "The Novels of George Meredith." In 1078, pp. 226-36.

1299 WRIGHT, Elizabeth Cox. "The Significance of Image Patterns in Meredith's *Modern Love." VN,* 13(1958), 1-9. (On *Rhoda Fleming.*)

1300 WRIGHT, Walter F. *Art and Substance in George Meredith.* Lincoln: U of Nebraska P, 1953.*†

Mitford, Mary Russell (1787–1855)

MAIN NOVEL

1301 *Our Village. Sketches of Rural Character and Scenery.* 5 vols. 1824–1832. [Originally appeared in *The Lady's Mag.*, 1819–1832.]

STUDIES

1302 MITFORD, Mary Russell. *Recollections of a Literary Life, or, Books, Places, and People.* 3 vols. London: Bentley, 1852.

1303 *The Life of Mary Russell Mitford Told by Herself in Her Letters to Her Friends.* Ed. A. G. L'Estrange. 3 vols. New York: Harper, 1870.

1304 ASTIN, Marjorie. *Mary Russell Mitford: Her Circle and Her Books.* London: Douglas, 1930.

1305 ROBERTS, W. J. *Mary Russell Mitford: The Tragedy of a Bluestocking.* London: Melrose, 1913.

1306 WATSON, Vera G. *Mary Russell Mitford.* London: Evans, 1949.

Morgan, Lady (née Sydney Owenson) (1783–1859)

MAIN NOVELS

1307 *St. Clair, or the Heiress of Desmond.* London, 1803. *The Wild Irish Girl.* 3 vols., 1806. *The O'Briens and the O'Flahertys: A National Tale.* 4 vols., 1827.

STUDIES

See 1670.

1308 *Lady Morgan's Memoirs: Autobiography, Diaries, and Correspondence.* Ed. W. Hepworth Dixon. 3 vols. Leipzig: Tauchnitz, 1863.

1309 FLANAGAN, Thomas B. "Lady Morgan." In 38, pp. 109-64.

1310 MORAUD, Marcel Ian. *Une Irlandaise libérale en France sous la Restauration, Lady Morgan.* Paris: Didier, 1954.

1311 STEVENSON, Lionel. *The Wild Irish Girl: The Life of Sydney Owenson, Lady Morgan.* London: Chapman & Hall, 1936.

Morier, James Justinian (1780–1849)

MAIN NOVELS

1312 *The Adventures of Hajji Baba of Ispahan.* 3 vols., 1824. *The Adventures of Hajji Baba of Ispahan in England.* 2 vols., 1828. *Zohrab the Hostage.* 3 vols., 1832. *Ayesha, the Maid of Kars.* 3 vols., 1834.

STUDIES

1313 *The Adventures of Hajji Baba in Ispahan.* Ed. Richard D. Altick. New York: Modern Library, 1954.

1314 MOUSSA-MAHMOUD, Fatma. "Orientals in Picaresque: A Chapter in the History of the Oriental Tale in England." *Cairo Studies in English,* 1961/62, pp. 145-88. (Discusses Hajji Baba.)

1315 SCOTT, Walter. Introduction to *EL* edition of *Hajji Baba.* [Originally a review in *QR,* 39(1829):73-96.]

Mulock, Dinah Maria, Later Mrs. Craik (1826–1887)

MAIN NOVELS

1316 *The Ogilvies.* 3 vols., 1849. *John Halifax, Gentleman.* 3 vols., 1856. *A Life for a Life.* 3 vols., 1859.

STUDY

1317 PARR, Louisa. *The Author of* John Halifax, Gentleman. *A Memoir.* London: Hurst & Blackett, 1898.

Oliphant, Margaret, née Wilson (1828–1897)

MAIN NOVELS

1318 From a total of nearly one hundred published titles: *Passages in the Life of Mrs. Margaret Maitland.* 3 vols., 1849. *Salem Chapel.* 2 vols., 1863. *The Rector and the Doctor's Family.* 3 vols., 1863. *The Perpetual Curate.* 3 vols., 1864. *Miss Marjoribanks.* 3 vols., 1866. *Phoebe, Junior: A Last Chronicle of Carlingford.* 3 vols., 1876. *A Beleaguered City,* 1880. *A Little Pilgrim in the Unseen,* 1882. *The Land of Darkness, along with Some Further Chapters in the Experience of the Little Pilgrims,* 1888.

STUDIES

1319 COLBY, Vineta, and Robert A. COLBY. "*A Beleaguered City:* A Fable for the Victorian Age." *NCF,* 16(1962):283-301.

1320 COLBY, Vineta, and Robert A. COLBY. *The Equivocal Virtue: Mrs. Oliphant and the Victorian Literary Market Place.* New York: Shoe String P, 1966.

1321 GWYNN, Stephen. *Saints and Scholars.* London: Butterworth, 1929.

1322 LEAVIS, Q. D. Introduction to *Miss Marjoribanks.* London: Chatto & Windus, 1969.

1323 MOORE, Katherine. "A Valiant Victorian." *Blackwood's*, 283(1958):231–43.

1324 WATSON, Kathleen. "George Eliot and Mrs. Oliphant: A Comparison in Social Attitudes." *EIC*, 19(1969):410–19.

"Ouida" (Marie Louise de la Ramée) (1839–1908)

MAIN NOVELS

1325 *Held in Bondage.* 3 vols., 1863. [First pub. in *New Monthly Mag.* as *Granville de Vigne: A Tale of the Day*, Jan. 1861–June 1863.] *Strathmore.* 3 vols., 1865. *Under Two Flags*, 1867. *Moths.* 3 vols., 1880. *In Maremma.* 3 vols., 1882.

STUDIES

See 62.

1326 BIGLAND, E. *Ouida: The Passionate Victorian.* London: Jarrolds, 1951.

1327 FFRENCH, Yvonne. *Ouida, a Study in Ostentation.* New York: Appleton, 1938.

1328 MANNING, Olivia. Introduction to *Under Two Flags.* New York: Stein & Day, 1969.

1329 STIRLING, Monica. *The Fine and the Wicked: The Life and Times of Ouida.* New York: Coward-McCann, 1957.

Pater, Walter (1839–1894)

NOVEL

1330 *Marius the Epicurean: His Sensations and Ideas.* 2 vols., 1885.

STUDIES

1331 BRZENK, Eugene. "The Unique Fictional World of Walter Pater." *NCF*, 13(1958):217–26.

1332 CECIL, Lord David. *The Fine Art of Reading and Other Literary Studies.* London: Constable, 1957.

1333 HOUGH, Graham. "Pater." *The Last Romantics.* London: Duckworth, 1947, pp. 134–74.*†

1334 KNOEPFLMACHER, U. C. "The 'Atmospheres' of *Marius the Epicurean*." See 187, pp. 189-223.*

1335 LANAGHAN, R. T. "Pattern in Walter Pater's Fiction." *SP*, 58(1961):69-91.

1336 MC KENZIE, Gordon. *The Literary Character of Walter Pater. UCPES* 32. Berkeley: U of California P, 1967.

1337 MONSMAN, Gerald Cornelius. *Pater's Portraits: Mythic Pattern in the Fiction of Walter Pater*. Baltimore: Johns Hopkins U P, 1967.

1338 ROSENBLATT, Louise M. "The Genesis of Pater's *Marius the Epicurean*." *CL*, 14(1963):242-60.

1339 SUDRANN, Jean. "Victorian Compromise and Modern Revolution." *ELH*, 26(1959):425-44. (On *Marius the Epicurean*.)

1340 VOGELER, Martha S. "The Religious Meaning of *Marius the Epicurean*." *NCF*, 19(1964):287-99.

Peacock, Thomas Love (1785-1866)

NOVELS

1341 *Headlong Hall*. London: Hookam, 1816. *Melincourt*. London: Hookam, 1817. *Nightmare Abbey*. London: Hookam, 1818. *Maid Marian*. London: Hookam, 1822. *The Misfortunes of Elphin*. London: Hookam, 1829. *Crotchet Castle*. London: Hookam, 1831. *Gryll Grange*. [*Fraser's Mag.*, 1860.] London, 1861.

BIBLIOGRAPHY AND COLLECTIONS

1342 *The Works of Thomas Love Peacock*. Halliford Edition. Ed. H. F. B. Brett-Smith and C. E. Jones. 10 vols. London: Constable; New York: Wells, 1924-1934. (Includes a biography by Brett-Smith.)*

1343 *Novels*. Ed. David Garnett. 2 vols. London: 1948.† (In U.S., only *Nightmare Abbey* and *Crotchet Castle* in paperback.)

1344 READ, Bill. "Thomas Love Peacock: An Enumerative Bibliography." *BB*, 24(1963-1964):32-4, 70-2, 88-91.

BIOGRAPHY

1345 CAMPBELL, Olwen Ward. *Thomas Love Peacock*. London: Barker, 1953.

1346 MAYOUX, Jean-Jacques. *Un Épicurien Anglais: Thomas Love Peacock*. Paris: Nizet et Bastard, 1937.

1347 PRIESTLEY, John B. *Thomas Love Peacock*. New York: Macmillan, 1927.

1348 VAN DOREN, Carl. *The Life of Thomas Love Peacock*. London, 1911; repr., New York: Russell & Russell, 1966.*

CRITICISM

See 608.

1349 ABLE, Augustus Henry. *Meredith and Peacock: A Study in Literary Influence*. Philadelphia: U of Pennsylvania P, 1933.

1350 BELL, Clive. *Pot-Boilers*. New York: Sunwise Turn, 1919.

1351 DAWSON, Carl. *Thomas Love Peacock*. London: Routledge & Kegan Paul, 1968.

1352 DYSON, A. E. "Peacock: The Wand of Enchantment." In his 450, pp. 57-71.

1353 GARNETT, Richard. *Essays of an Ex-Librarian*. London: Heinemann, 1901.

1354 PRICE, J. B. "Thomas Love Peacock." *ContempR*, 181(1952):365-9.

1355 PRIESTLEY, John B. *The English Comic Characters*. London: Lane, 1928, pp. 178-97.†

1356 RYAN, Mariana. "The Peacockian Essence." *BUSE*, 3(1957):231-42.

1357 SALY, Paulina J. "Peacock's Use of Music in His Novels." *JEGP*, 54(1955):370-9.

1358 STEUERT, H. "Thomas Love Peacock." *DubR*, 216(1945):67-74.

Reade, Charles (1814-1884)

NOVELS

1359 *Peg Woffington*. London: Bentley, 1853. *Christie Johnstone*. London: Bentley, 1853. *It is Never Too Late to Mend: A Matter of Fact Romance*. 3 vols. London: Bentley, 1856. *White Lies*. [*London Journal*, 1857.] 3 vols. London: Bentley 1857. *"Love Me Little, Love Me Long."* 2 vols. London: Trubner, 1859. *The Cloister and the Hearth: A Tale of the Middle Ages*. 4 vols. London: Trubner, 1861. *Hard Cash: A Matter of Fact Romance*. [In *All the Year Round* as "Very Hard Cash," 1863.] 3 vols. London: Low & Marston, 1863. *Griffith Gaunt; or, Jealousy*. [*The Argosy*, 1866.] 3 vols. London: Chapman & Hall, 1867. *Foul Play*. [*Once a Week*, 1868.] 3 vols. London: Bradbury & Evans, 1868. *Put Yourself in His Place*. [*Cornhill Mag.*, 1870.] 3 vols. London: Smith, Elder, 1870. *A Terrible Temptation*. [*Cassell's Mag.*, 1871.] 3 vols. London: Chapman & Hall, 1871. *A Simpleton: A Story of the Day*. [*London Society*.] 3 vols. London: Chatto & Windus, 1873. *A Woman Hater*. 3 vols. Edinburgh and London: Blackwood, 1877. *A Perilous Secret*. [*Temple Bar Mag.*, 1884.] 2 vols. London: Bentley, 1884.

BIBLIOGRAPHY, COLLECTIONS, EDITIONS

See 22, 25,* 1367.

1360 *Novels*. Library Edition. 13 vols. London: Chatto & Windus, 1901-1910.

1361 CORDASCO, Francesco, and Kenneth SCOTT. *Wilkie Collins and Charles Reade: A Bibliography of Critical Notices and Studies.* Brooklyn: Long Island U P, 1949.

1362 PARRISH, Morris L. *Wilkie Collins and Charles Reade.* London: Constable, 1940. (List and description of first editions.)

1363 SUTCLIFFE, Emerson Grant. "Charles Reade's Notebooks." *SP,* 27(1930):64–109.

1364 BURNS, Wayne. "More Reade Notebooks." *SP,* 42(1945):824–42.

BIOGRAPHY

See 61.

1365 ELWIN, Malcolm. *Charles Reade, a Biography.* London: Cape, 1931.

1366 READE, Charles L., and Compton READE. *Charles Reade, A Memoir.* 2 vols. New York: Harper, 1887.

1367 RIVES, Léone. *Charles Reade: sa vie, ses romans.* Toulouse: Imprimerie toulousaine, 1940. (Includes a comprehensive bibliography.)*

CRITICAL

See 4,* 13.

1368 BOOTH, Bradford A. "Trollope, Reade, and *Shilly-Shally.*" *Trollopian,* 1(1947):45–54; 2:43–51.

1369 BURNS, Wayne. *Charles Reade: A Study in Victorian Authorship.* New York: Bookman, 1961.*

1370 BURNS, Wayne. "Pre-Raphaelitism in Charles Reade's Early Fiction." *PMLA,* 60(1945):1149–64.

1371 BURNS, Wayne. "The Sheffield Flood: A Critical Study of Charles Reade's Fiction." *PMLA,* 63(1948):686–95.

1372 HAINES, Lewis F. "Reade, Mill, and Zola: A Study of the Character and Intention of Charles Reade's Realistic Method." *SP,* 40(1943):463–80.

1373 ORWELL, George. "Books in General." *New Statesman and Nation,* 20(1940):162.

1374 SMITH, Sheila M. "Propaganda and Hard Facts in Charles Reade's Didactic Novels." *RMS,* 4(1960):135–49. (Study of *It Is Never Too Late to Mend* and *Hard Cash.*)

1375 SUTCLIFFE, Emerson Grant. "Charles Reade in His Heroes." *Trollopian* (see 18) 1(1946):3–15.

1376 SUTCLIFFE, Emerson Grant. "Fact, Realism and Morality in Reade's Fiction." *SP,* 41(1944):582–98.

1377 SUTCLIFFE, Emerson Grant. "*Foemina Vera* in Charles Reade's Novels." *PMLA,* 46(1931):1260–79.

1378 SUTCLIFFE, Emerson Grant. "Plotting in Reade's Novels." *PMLA,* 47(1932):834–63.

1379 SUTCLIFFE, Emerson Grant. "Psychological Presentation in Reade's Novels." *SP*, 38(1941):521–42.

1380 SUTCLIFFE, Emerson Grant. "The Stage in Reade's Novels." *SP*, 27(1930):654–88.

1381 SUTCLIFFE, Emerson Grant. "Unique and Repeated Situations and Themes in Reade's Fiction." *PMLA*, 60(1945):1149–64.

1382 SUTCLIFFE, Emerson Grant, and Wayne BURNS. "*Uncle Tom* and Charles Reade." *AL*, 17(1946):334–7.

THE CLOISTER AND THE HEARTH

1383 *The Cloister and the Hearth*. Ed. C. B. Wheeler. London and New York: Oxford U P, 1910, 1915.*

1384 BOOTH, Bradford A. Introduction to *The Cloister and the Hearth*. New York: Harper, 1961.†

1385 BURNS, Wayne. "*The Cloister and the Hearth*: A Classic Reconsidered." *NCF*, 2(1947):71–81.

1386 SWINBURNE, A. C. Introduction to *The Cloister and the Hearth*. EL. New York: Dutton, 1915.

1387 TURNER, Albert Morton. *The Making of "The Cloister and the Hearth."* Chicago: U of Chicago P, 1938.

Reid, Thomas Mayne (1818–1883)

SOME NOVELS

1388 *The Rifle Rangers*. 3 vols., 1850. *The Plant Hunters*, 1857. *The Headless Horseman*. 2 vols., 1866. *Gaspar the Gaucho*, 1874. *No Quarter*. 3 vols., 1888.

STUDY

1389 REID, Elizabeth. *Captain Mayne Reid. His Life and Adventures*. London: Greening, 1900. [By Elizabeth Reid, his widow, assisted by C. H. Coe.]

Ritchie, Lady

See below, under THACKERAY, ANNE ISABELLA.

"Rutherford, Mark" (William Hale White) (1831-1913)

MAIN NOVELS

1390 *The Autobiography of Mark Rutherford, Dissenting Minister*, 1881. *Mark Rutherford's Deliverance, Being the Second Part of his Autobiography*, 1885. *The Revolution in Tanner's Lane*, 1887. *Catharine Furze*. 2 vols., 1893. *Clara Hopgood*, 1896.

STUDIES

1391 NOWELL-SMITH, S. *Mark Rutherford: A Bibliography of the First Editions*. London: Bookman's Journal, 1930.

1392 DAVIS, W. Eugene. "William Hale White ('Mark Rutherford'): An Annotated Bibliography of Writings about Him." *ELT*, 10(1967):97-117; 150-60; 11(1968):64-5.

1393 *Pages from a Journal, with Other Papers*. London: Unwin, 1900.

1394 *More Pages from a Journal*. London: Frowde, 1910.

1395 *Last Pages from a Journal*. Ed. D. V. White. London and New York: Oxford U P, 1915. (Published posthumously.)

1396 MAC LEAN, C. M. *Mark Rutherford*. London: Macdonald, 1955.

1397 MERTON, Stephen. *Mark Rutherford*. TEAS. New York: Twayne, 1967.

1398 SALGADO, Gamini. "The Rhetoric of Sincerity: *The Autobiography of Mark Rutherford* as Fiction." *Renaissance and Modern Essays Presented to Vivian de Sola Pinto in Celebration of His Seventieth Birthday*. London: Routledge & Kegan Paul, 1966, 159-68.

1399 STOCK, Irvin. *William Hale White (Mark Rutherford): A Critical Study*. New York: Columbia U P, 1956.

1400 STONE, Wilfred H. *Religion and Art of William Hale White*. Stanford: Stanford U P, 1954.*

1401 TAYLOR, A. E. "The Novels of Mark Rutherford." *E&S*, 5(1914):51-74.

1402 THOMSON, Patricia. "The Novels of Mark Rutherford." *EIC*, 14(1964):256-67.

1403 WILLEY, Basil. " 'Mark Rutherford.' " See 134, pp. 186-247.*

Sala, George Augustus Henry (1828-1896)

SOME NOVELS

1404 *How I Tamed Mrs. Cruiser. By Benedict Cruiser*. London: Ackerman, 1858. *The Seven Sons of Mammon*. 3 vols., 1862. *The Story of the Count de Chambord. A Trilogy*, 1873.

STUDY

1405 STRAUS, Ralph. *Sala: The Portrait of an Eminent Victorian*. London: Constable, 1942.

Savage, Marmion W. (1803–1872)

MAIN NOVELS

1406 *The Falcon Family; or, Young Ireland*, 1845. *The Bachelor of Albany*, 1847. *Reuben Medlicott; or, The Coming Man*, 1852.

Scott, Sir Walter (1771–1832)

NOVELS

1407 *Waverley; or, 'Tis Sixty Years Since*. 3 vols. Edinburgh: Ballantyne & Constable, 1814. *Guy Mannering; or, The Astrologer*. 3 vols. Edinburgh: Ballantyne & Constable, 1815. *The Antiquary*. 3 vols. Edinburgh: Ballantyne, 1816. *The Black Dwarf*. Edinburgh: Blackwood, 1816. [As Vol. I of *Tales of My Landlord*.] *Old Mortality*. Edinburgh: Blackwood, 1816. [As Vols. II–IV of *Tales of My Landlord*.] *The Search after Happiness; or, The Quest of the Sultan of Serendib*. [*The Sale Room*, nos. 1–28.] Edinburgh: Jan.–July 1817.

The Heart of Mid-Lothian. 4 vols. Edinburgh: Constable, 1818. [As Second Series of *Tales of My Landlord*.] *Rob Roy*. 3 vols. Edinburgh: Ballantyne, 1818. *The Bride of Lammermoor*. Edinburgh: Constable, 1819. [As part of Third Series of *Tales of My Landlord*.] *A Legend of Montrose*. Edinburgh: Constable, 1819. [As part of Third Series of *Tales of My Landlord*.] *Ivanhoe. A Romance*. 3 vols. Edinburgh: Constable, 1820. *The Monastery: A Romance*. 3 vols. Edinburgh: Ballantyne, 1820. *The Abbot*. 3 vols. Edinburgh: Ballantyne & Constable, 1820. *Kenilworth: A Romance*. 4 vols. Edinburgh: Ballantyne & Constable, 1821. *The Pirate*. 3 vols. Edinburgh: Constable, 1822. *The Fortunes of Nigel*. 4 vols. Edinburgh: Constable, 1822. *Peveril of the Peak*. 4 vols. Edinburgh: Constable, 1822. *Quentin Durward*. 3 vols. Edinburgh: Constable, 1822. *St. Ronan's Well*. 3 vols. Edinburgh: Constable, 1824. *Redgauntlet: A Tale of the Eighteenth Century*. 3 vols. Edinburgh: Constable, 1824. *The Betrothed*. 2 vols. Edinburgh: Constable, 1825. [As part of *Tales of the Crusaders*.] *The Talisman*. 2 vols. Edinburgh: Constable, 1825. [As part of *Tales of the Crusaders*.] *Woodstock; or, The Cavalier*. 3 vols. Edinburgh: Constable, 1826. *The Highland Widow*. Edinburgh: Cadell, 1827. [As part of *Chronicles of the Canongate*.] *The Two Drovers*. Edinburgh: Cadell, 1827. [As part of *Chronicles of the Canongate*.] *The Surgeon's Daughter*. Edinburgh: Cadell, 1827. [As part of *Chronicles of the Canongate*.] *St. Valentine's Day; or, The Fair Maid of Perth*. Edinburgh: Cadell, 1828. [Second Series of *Chronicles of the Canongate*.] *Anne of Geierstein; or, The Maiden of the Mist*. Edinburgh: Cadell, 1829. *Count Robert of Paris*. Edinburgh: Cadell, 1832. [As part of Series Four of *Tales of My Landlord*.] *Castle Dangerous*. Edinburgh: Cadell, 1832. [As part of Series Four of *Tales of My Landlord*.]

BIBLIOGRAPHY AND REFERENCE

1409 BURN, Allston. *Sir Walter Scott: An Index Placing the Short Poems in His Novels and in His Long Poems and Dramas.* Cambridge, Mass.: Harvard U P, 1936.

1410 CORSON, J. C. *A Bibliography of Sir Walter Scott: A Classified and Annotated List of Books and Articles . . ., 1797-1940.* London: Oliver & Boyd, 1943.

1411 CORSON, J. C. "Scott Studies I" and "Scott Studies II." *EdinUJ,* 18(1955-1956):23-32, 104-13.

1412 HILLHOUSE, J. T. "Sir Walter Scott." *English Romantic Poets and Essayists.* Ed. C. W. Houtchens and L. H. Houtchens. New York: Modern Language Association, 1957.*

1413 HUSBAND, Margaret F. A. *A Dictionary of the Characters in the Waverly Novels of Sir Walter Scott* [1910]. New York: Humanities, 1962.

1414 WORTHINGTON, Greville. *A Bibliography of the Waverley Novels.* New York: Smith, 1931.

COLLECTED EDITIONS, LETTERS, AND JOURNALS

THE WAVERLEY NOVELS

A scholarly edition is now in preparation (ed. by J. C. Corson). Apart from Scott's own Collected Edition (48 vols., 1829-1833, "The Magnum," with his copious prefaces and appendices on sources and background), the following, among many collected editions, may be mentioned:

1415 *The Waverley Novels.* Dryburgh Edition. 25 vols. Edinburgh: Black, 1892-1894.

1416 GRIERSON, H. J. C., et al., eds. *The Letters of Sir Walter Scott.* 12 vols. London: Constable, 1932-1937.*

1417 PARTINGTON, Wilfrid, ed. *The Private Letter-Books of Sir Walter Scott.* New York: Stokes, 1930.

1418 TAIT, J. G., and W. M. PARKER, eds. *The Journal of Sir Walter Scott.* 3 vols. Edinburgh: Oliver & Boyd, 1939-1947. Single vol. ed., Edinburgh and London: Oliver & Boyd, 1950.*

BIOGRAPHICAL

1419 BUCHAN, John. *Sir Walter Scott.* London and Toronto: Cassell, 1932.

1420 CARSWELL, Donald. *Scott and His Circle.* Garden City, N.Y.: Doubleday, Doran, 1930. [British ed. has title: *Sir Walter.*]

1421 CHANDLER, Alice. "Sir Walter Scott and the Medieval Revival." *NCF,* 19(1965):315-32.

1422 CRAWFORD, Thomas. *Scott.* Writers and Critics. Edinburgh and London: Oliver & Boyd, 1965.

1423 FRENCH, Richard. "The Religion of Sir Walter Scott." *SSL,* 2(1964):32-44.

1424 GRIERSON, Herbert J. C. *Sir Walter Scott, Bart.: A New Life Supplementary to and Corrective of Lockhart's Biography.* London: Constable, 1938.*

1425 GWYNN, Stephen L. *The Life of Sir Walter Scott.* London: Butterworth, 1930.

1426 HART, F. R. "*The Fair Maid,* Manzoni's *Betrothed,* and the Grounds of Waverley Criticism." *NCF,* 18(1962):103–18.

1427 JOHNSON, Edgar. *Sir Walter Scott: The Great Unknown.* 2 vols. New York: Macmillan, 1970.*

1428 KEITH, Christine. *The Author of* Waverley: *A Study in the Personality of Sir Walter Scott.* London: Hale, 1964.

1429 KER, William Paton. *Sir Walter Scott.* Glasgow: Maclehose, Jackson, 1919.

1430 LANG, Andrew. *Sir Walter Scott.* New York: Scribner's, 1906.*

1431 LOCKHART, J. G. *Memoirs of the Life of Sir Walter Scott, Bart.* 10 vols. Edinburgh: Cadell, 1839. (Many later expanded editions.)*

1432 PEARSON, Hesketh. *Sir Walter Scott: His Life and Personality.* New York: Harper, 1955.

1433 POPE-HENNESSY, Una. *Sir Walter Scott.* London: Home & Van Thal, 1948.

1434 SAINTSBURY, George. *Sir Walter Scott.* London: Oliphant, Anderson & Ferrier, 1897.

CRITICISM

1435 BAGEHOT, Walter. "The Waverley Novels." *Literary Studies.* 4th ed. 2 vols. London: Longmans, Green, 1891. (In EL, 2 vols., 1932.)

1436 BALL, Margaret. *Sir Walter Scott as a Critic of Literature.* New York: Columbia U P, 1907.

1437 BUSHNELL, Nelson S. "Scott's Mature Achievement as a Novelist of Manners." *SSL,* 3(1965):3–29.

1438 CROCKETT, W. S. *The Scott Originals: An Account of Notables and Worthies, the Originals of Characters in the Waverley Novels.* 3d ed. Edinburgh: Grant & Murray, 1932.

1439 CRUTTWELL, Patrick. *Walter Scott.* In 39, Vol. V, pp. 104–111.*

1440 DAICHES, David. "Scott's Achievement as a Novelist." *NCF,* 6(1951):81–95, 153–73.

1441 DAVIE, Donald. *The Heyday of Sir Walter Scott.* London: Routledge & Kegan Paul, 1961. (Largely on Scott's disciples, Pushkin, Mickiewicz, Maria Edgeworth, and Fenimore Cooper.)*

1442 FISKE, Christabel T. *Epic Suggestion in the Imagery of the Waverley Novels.* New Haven: Yale U P, 1940.

1443 GOLDSTONE, Herbert. "The Question of Scott." *EJ,* 46(1957):187–95.

1444 GOOCH, G. P. "Historical Novels." *EDH,* 23(1947):53–71.

1445 GRIERSON, Sir Herbert J. C. *Sir Walter Scott Today.* London: Constable, 1932.

1446 GRIERSON, Sir Herbert J. C., et al. *Sir Walter Scott Lectures, 1940-1948.* Edinburgh: Edinburgh U P, 1951. (Lectures given at Edinburgh University. Later lectures repr. in *Edinburgh University Journal.*)*

1447 HABER, Thomas B. "The Chapter Tags in the *Waverley Novels.*" *PMLA*, 45(1930):1140-9.

1448 HART, F. R. *Scott's Novels: The Plotting of Historic Survival.* Charlottesville: U of Virginia P, 1966.

1449 HAZLITT, William. "On the English Novelists"; "The Spirit of the Age"; "Why the Heroes of Romance are Insipid." *Complete Works of William Hazlitt.* Ed. P. P. Howe. 21 vols. London and Toronto: Dent, 1930-1934.*

1450 HILLHOUSE, J. T. *The Waverley Novels and Their Critics.* Minneapolis: U of Minnesota P, 1936.*

1451 JACK, Ian. *Sir Walter Scott.* WTW. London and New York: Longmans, Green, 1958.†

1452 KROEBER, Karl. "The Narrative Pattern of Scott." *Romantic Narrative Art.* Madison: U of Wisconsin P, 1960, pp. 168-87.†

1453 LANDIS, Paul. "*The Waverley Novels;* or, a Hundred Years After." *PMLA*, 52(1937):461-73.

1454 LAUBER, John. "Scott on the Art of Fiction." *SEL*, 3(1963):543-54.

1455 MACINTYRE, D. C. "Scott and the Waverley Novels." *REL*, 7(1966):9-19.

1456 MAYO, R. D. "The Chronology of the Waverley Novels: The Evidence of the Manuscripts." *PMLA*, 63(1948):935-49.

1457 MOORE, J. R. "Defoe and Scott." *PMLA*, 56(1941):710-35.

1458 MUIR, Edwin. *Scott and Scotland.* London: Routledge, 1936.*

1459 NEEDLER, G. H. *Goethe and Scott.* Toronto: Oxford U P, 1951.

1460 ORIANS, G. H. "Walter Scott, Mark Twain, and the Civil War." *SAQ*, 40(1941):342-59. (Demolishes Twain's view that Scott was a cause of the Civil War.)

1461 PARSONS, C. O. *Witchcraft and Demonology in Scott's Fiction with Chapters on the Supernatural in Scottish Literature.* Edinburgh and London: Oliver & Boyd, 1964.*

1462 RALEIGH, John Henry. "What Scott Meant to the Victorians." *VS*, 8(1963):7-34. Repr. in his *Time, Place and Idea* (127).

1463 ROBERTS, Paul. "Sir Walter Scott's Contributions to the English Vocabulary." *PMLA*, 68(1953):189-210.

1464 *Scott Centenary Articles.* London: Oxford U P, 1932. (Essays on many of the novels by various hands including Thomas Seccombe, W. P. Ker, and George Gordon.)

1465 SENIOR, Nassau. "Sir Walter Scott." In 92, pp. 1-188.

1466 SMITH, J. C. "Scott and Shakespeare." *E&S*, 24(1939):114-31.

1467 STEPHEN, Leslie. "Sir Walter Scott." *Hours in a Library*. London: Smith, Elder, 1899, vol. I, pp. 137-68.

1468 TILLYARD, E. M. W. "Scott." *The Epic Strain in the English Novel*. London: Chatto & Windus, 1958. (Especially on *Waverley, Old Mortality, Rob Roy*, pp. 59-116.)

1469 VERRALL, A. W. "The Prose of Walter Scott." *Collected Literary Essays*. Cambridge: Cambridge U P, 1913.

1470 WELSH, Alexander. *The Hero of the Waverley Novels*. New Haven: Yale U P, 1963.

1471 WOOLF, Virginia. "Sir Walter Scott. I, Gas at Abbotsford. II, *The Antiquary*." *The Moment and Other Essays*. London: Hogarth, 1947, pp. 50-59.

See 1464.

BRIDE OF LAMMERMOOR

1472 GORDON, Robert C. "*The Bride of Lammermoor*: A Novel of Tory Pessimism." *NCF*, 12(1957):110-24.

1473 OWEN, E. "Critics of *The Bride of Lammermoor*." *DR*, 18(1938):365-71.

1474 PARSONS, Coleman O. "The Dalrymple Legend in *The Bride of Lammermoor*." *RES*, 19(1943):51-8.

THE HEART OF MIDLOTHIAN

See 48, Kettle, 71,* Pritchett, 87,* Van Ghent, 98,* 192, and Davie, 1441.

1475 *The Heart of Midlothian*. Ed. John Henry Raleigh. Boston: Houghton Mifflin, 1966.†

1476 BIGGINS, D. "*Measure for Measure* and *The Heart of Midlothian*." *EA*, 14(1961):193-205.

1477 CRAIG, David. "*The Heart of Midlothian*: Its Religious Basis." *EIC*, 8(1958):217-25. See also 174, pp. 166-97.*

1478 FISHER, P. F. "Providence, Fate, and the Historical Imagination in Scott's *The Heart of Midlothian*." *NCF*, 10(1955):99-114.

1479 LYNSKEY, Winifred. "The Drama of the Elect and the Reprobate in Scott's *Heart of Midlothian*." *BUSE*, 4(1960):39-48.

1480 MARSHALL, W. H. "Point of View and Structure in *The Heart of Midlothian*." *NCF*, 16(1961):257-62.

1481 MAYHEAD, Robin. "*The Heart of Midlothian*: Scott as Artist." *EIC*, 6(1956):266-77.

REDGAUNTLET

See 58.

1482 DAICHES, David. "Scott's *Redgauntlet*." In 88, pp. 46-59.*

1483 DEVLIN, D. D. "Scott and *Redgauntlet*." *REL*, 4(1963):91-103.

WAVERLEY

See Davie, 1441,* 1468.

1484 *Waverley.* Ed. Edgar Johnson. New York: New American Library, 1964. (Annotated.)†

1485 GORDON, S. Stewart. "*Waverley* and the Unified Design." *ELH*, 8(1951):107-22.

1486 RALEIGH, John H. "*Waverley* and *The Fair Maid of Perth.*" *Some British Romantics.* Eds. James V. Logan, John E. Gordon, and Northrop Frye. Columbus: Ohio State U P, 1966, 235-66.

ON OTHER INDIVIDUAL NOVELS (Alphabetically by novel)

See 1441, (on *Rob Roy*), 1468.

1487 DUNCAN, Joseph E. "The Anti-Romantic in *Ivanhoe.*" *NCF*, 9(1955):293-300.

1488 ROSENBERG, Edgar. "The Jew as Clown and the Jew's Daughter." In 205, pp. 73-115. (On *Ivanhoe.*)

1489 *Old Mortality.* Ed. with introduction by Alexander Welsh. Boston: Houghton Mifflin, 1967.†

1490 *Rob Roy.* Ed. Edgar Johnson. Boston: Houghton Mifflin, 1956.†

1491 CADBURY, William. "The Two Structures of *Rob Roy.*" *MLQ*, 29(1968):42-60.

1492 PIKE, B. A. "Scott as Pessimist: A View of *St. Ronan's Well.*" *REL*, 7(1966):29-38.

Shelley, Mary Wollstonecraft, née Godwin (1797–1851)

MAIN NOVELS

1493 *Frankenstein, or the Modern Prometheus.* London: Lackingham, Hughes, Harding, Mavor & Jones, 1818. *Valperga.* London: Whittaker, 1823. *The Last Man.* London: Colburn, 1826. *Lodore.* London: Bentley, 1835.

LETTERS AND JOURNALS

1494 JONES, Frederick L. "Mary Shelley to Maria Gisborne: New Letters," *SP*, 52(1955):37-74.

1495 JONES, Frederick L., ed. *The Letters of Mary W. Shelley.* 2 vols. Norman: U of Oklahoma P, 1944.

1496 JONES, Frederick L., ed. *Mary Shelley's Journal.* Norman: U of Oklahoma P, 1947.

1497 SPARK, Muriel, and Derek STANFORD. *My Best Mary: The Selected Letters of Mary Wollstonecraft Shelley.* London: Wingate, 1953.

BIOGRAPHICAL

1498   BIGLAND, Eileen. *Mary Shelley*. New York: Appleton-Century-Crofts, 1959.

1499   GRYLLS, Rosalie Glynn. *Mary Shelley: A Biography*. London and New York: Oxford U P, 1938.

1500   NITCHIE, Elizabeth. *Mary Shelley: Author of* Frankenstein. New Brunswick: Rutgers U P, 1953.

1501   SPARK, Muriel. *Child of Light, a Reassessment of Mary Wollstonecraft Shelley*. Hadleigh, Essex: Tower Bridge, 1951.*

CRITICAL

1502   *Frankenstein*. Ed. Elizabeth Nitchie. Chapel Hill: U of North Carolina P, 1959.

1503   *The Last Man*. Ed. H. J. Luke, Jr. Lincoln: U of Nebraska P, 1965.†

1504   BLOOM, Harold. "*Frankenstein*, or the New Prometheus." *PR*, 32(1965):611–18.

1505   GOLDBERG, M. A. "Moral and Myth in Mrs. Shelley's *Frankenstein*." *Keats-Shelley Journal*, 8(1959):27–38.

1506   LOVELL, Ernest, Jr. "Byron and the Byronic Hero in the Novels of Mary Shelley." *UTSE*, 30(1951):158–83.

1507   LUKE, Hugh J., Jr. "*The Last Man*: Mary Shelley's Myth of the Solitary." *Prairie Schooner*, 39(1966):316–27.

1508   LUND, Mary Graham. "Mary Godwin Shelley and the Monster." *UKCR*, 28(1962):253–8.

1509   PECK, W. E. "The Biographical Elements in the Novels of Mary Wollstonecraft Shelley." *PMLA*, 38(1923):196–219.

1510   POLLIN, Burton R. "Philosophical and Literary Sources of *Frankenstein*." *CL*, 17(1965):97–108.

1511   RIEGER, James. "Dr. Polidori and the Genesis of *Frankenstein*." *SEL*, 3(1963):461–72.

Sherwood, Mary Martha, née Butt (1771-1851)

MAIN NOVELS *(out of some 55.)*

1512   *The Tradition*, 1794. *The History of the Fairchild Family; or, The Child's Manual*, 1818-1867. *The Lady of the Manor*. 4 vols., 1825-1829. *The Flowers of the Forest*, 1839. *Boys Will Be Boys*. By Mrs. Sherwood and her daughter, 1854.

STUDIES

1513   *The Life and Times of Mrs. Sherwood. From the Diaries of Captain and Mrs. Sherwood*. Ed. F. J. H. Darton. London: Gardner, Darton, 1910.

1514 KELLY, Sophia. *Life of Mrs. Sherwood.* London: Darton, 1854.

1515 SMITH, Naomi Gladys Royde. *The State of Mind of Mrs. Sherwood.* London: Macmillan, 1946.

Shorthouse, Joseph Henry (1834-1903)

MAIN NOVELS

1516 *John Inglesant. A Romance,* 1880. *The Little Schoolmaster Mark: A Spiritual Romance,* 1883-1884. *Sir Percival: A Story of the Past and Present,* 1886. *The Countess Eve,* 1888.

STUDIES

1517 SHORTHOUSE, Sarah, ed. *The Life, Letters and Literary Remains of J. H. Shorthouse.* 2 vols. London: Macmillan, 1905.

See 167.

1518 BISHOP, Marchard. "*John Inglesant* and Its Author." *EDH,* 29(1958):73-86.

1519 HOUGH, Graham. "Books in General." *New Statesman and Nation,* Aug. 3, 1946, pp. 83-4.

1520 MORE, Paul Elmer. "J. Henry Shorthouse." *Shelburne Essays, Third Series.* New York and London: Putnam, 1905, pp. 213-43.

1521 POLAK, Meijer. *The Historical, Philosophical and Religious Aspects of John Inglesant.* Purmerend, The Netherlands: Muusses, 1933.

Stevenson, Robert Louis (1850-1894)

NOVELS

1522 *Treasure Island.* [First pub. in modified form in *Young Folks,* Oct. 1, 1881-Jan. 28, 1882, as by "Captain George North."] London: Cassell, 1883. *Prince Otto. A Romance.* [First pub. in *Longman's Mag.,* April-Oct. 1885.] London: Chatto & Windus, 1885. *Strange Case of Dr. Jekyll and Mr. Hyde.* London: Longmans, Green, 1886. *Kidnapped: Being Memoirs of the Adventures of David Balfour in the Year 1751.* [First pub. in *Young Folks,* May 1-July 13, 1886.] London: James Henderson, 1886. *The Black Arrow: A Tale of the Two Roses.* [First pub. in *Young Folks,* June 30-Oct. 20, 1883, as by "Captain North."] London: Cassell, 1888.

1523   *The Master of Ballantrae.* [First pub. in *Scribner's Mag.*, Aug. 1891–July 1892.] London: Cassell, 1889. *The Wrong Box.* [With Lloyd Osbourne.] London: Longmans, Green, 1889. *The Wrecker.* [With Lloyd Osbourne.] [First pub. in *Scribner's Mag.*, Aug. 1891–July 1892.] London: Cassell, 1892. *Catriona. A Sequel to* Kidnapped. [First pub. in *Atalanta*, Dec. 1892–Sept. 1893, as *David Balfour: Memoirs of His Adventures at Home and Abroad.*] London: Cassell, 1893. *The Ebb-Tide: A Trio and Quartette.* [With Lloyd Osbourne.] [First pub. in *To-day*, Nov. 11, 1893–Feb. 3, 1894.] London: Heinemann, 1894. *Weir of Hermiston. An Unfinished Romance.* [First pub. in *Cosmopolis*, Jan.-April 1896. Not completed.] London: Chatto & Windus, 1896. *St. Ives: Being the Adventures of a French Prisoner in England.* [First pub. in *Pall Mall Mag.*, Nov. 1896–Nov. 1897.] New York: Scribner's, 1897.

BIBLIOGRAPHY

1524   EHRSAM, T. G., R. H. DEILY, and R. M. SMITH, eds. In 8, pp. 228–63.

1525   MC KAY, George L., ed. *A Stevenson Library Catalogue of a Collection of Writings by and about Robert Louis Stevenson.* 6 vols. New Haven: Yale U P, 1952. (Includes letters to and by Stevenson.)

1526   PRIDEAUX, W. F., and Mrs. Luther S. LIVINGSTON, eds. *A Bibliography of the Works of Robert Louis Stevenson.* London: Hollings, 1917.

COLLECTIONS, LETTERS, ETC.

1527   *Works.* 32 vols. New York: Scribner's, 1925. (Very numerous paperbacks of novels and short stories. Good representation in "Selected Writings" [Modern Library Giant.])

1528   COLVIN, Sidney, ed. *Letters.* 5 vols. London: Heinemann, 1924.

1529   FERGUSON, J. DeLancey, and Marshall WAINGROW, eds. *RLS: Stevenson's Letters to Charles Baxter.* New Haven: Yale U P, 1956.

1530   SMITH, Janet A., ed. *Henry James and Stevenson.* New York: Macmillan, 1949.*

BIOGRAPHICAL AND GENERAL

1531   BALFOUR, Graham. *The Life of Robert Louis Stevenson.* New York: Scribner's, 1915.

1532   BENSON, E. F. "The Myth of Robert Louis Stevenson." *London Mercury*, 12(1925):268–83, 372–84.

1533   BONDS, Robert E. "*The Mystery of Ballantrae.*" *ELT*, 7(1964):8–11.

1534   BUTTS, Dennis. *R. L. Stevenson.* New York: Walck, 1966.

1535   CARRÉ, Jean Marie. *The Frail Warrior.* Trans. Eleanor Hard. New York: Coward-McCann, 1930.

1536   CHAPMAN, John Jay. "Robert Louis Stevenson." *Emerson and Other Essays.* New York: Scribner's, 1898.

1537   CHESTERTON, G. K. *Robert Louis Stevenson.* New York: Dodd, Mead, 1928.

1538 DAICHES, David. *Robert Louis Stevenson*. Norfolk, Conn.: New Directions, 1947.*

1539 EGAN, Joseph J. "From History to Myth: A Symbolic Reading of *The Master of Ballantrae*." *SEL*, 8(1968):699-710.

1540 EIGNER, Edwin M. *Robert Louis Stevenson and Romantic Tradition*. Princeton: Princeton U P, 1966.

1541 ELWIN, Malcolm. *The Strange Case of Robert Louis Stevenson*. London: Macdonald, 1950.

1542 FIEDLER, Leslie A. "R. L. S. Revisited." *No! in Thunder*. Boston: Beacon, 1960, pp. 77-92.*

1543 FURNAS, J. C. *Voyage to Windward: The Life of Robert Louis Stevenson*. New York: Sloane, 1951. (Selected bibliography.)†

1544 KIELY, Robert. *Robert Louis Stevenson and the Fiction of Adventure*. Cambridge, Mass.: Harvard U P, 1964.*

1545 KILROY, James F. "Narrative Techniques in *The Master of Ballantrae*. *SSL*, 5(1968):98-106.

1546 MIYOSHI, Masao. "Dr. Jekyll and the Emergence of Mr. Hyde." *CE*, 27(1966):470-4, 479-80.

1547 SMITH, Janet A. *R. L. Stevenson*. London: Duckworth, 1937.

1548 STEPHEN, Leslie. *Studies of a Biographer*. New York: Putnam, 1907, Vol. IV, pp. 191-229.

1549 SWINNERTON, Frank. *Robert Louis Stevenson: A Critical Study*. London: Doran, 1914.

Surtees, Robert Smith (1803-1864)

MAIN NOVELS

1550 *Jorrock's Jaunts and Jollities, or the Hunting, Racing, Driving, Sailing, Eating, Eccentric and Extravagant Exploits of that Renowned Sporting Citizen, Mr. John Jorrocks*. [First appeared in *The New Sporting Mag.*, 1831-1834.] 1838. *Handley Cross, or, The Spa Hunt: A Sporting Tale*. 3 vols., 1843. *Hillingdon Hall, or, the Cockney Squire: A Tale of Country Life*. 3 vols., 1843. *Hawbuck Grange, or, The Sporting Adventures of Thomas Scott, Esq.*, 1847. *Mr. Sponge's Sporting Tour*, 1853. *Ask Mamma, or, The Richest Commoner in England*, 1858. *Plain or Ringlets?*, 1860. *Mr. Romford's Hounds*, 1865.

STUDIES

See 1712.

1551 COLLISON, Robert L. *A Jorrocks Handbook*. London: Coole Book Service, 1964.

1552 COOPER, Leonard. *R. S. Surtees*. London: Baker, 1952.

1553 CUMING, E. D. *Robert Smith Surtees, Creator of Jorrocks, 1803-1864*. London: Scribner's, 1924.

1554 DOBRÉE, Bonamy. "Robert Smith Surtees." In 699, pp. 57-71.

1555 HOYT, Charles A. "Robert Smith Surtees." *Minor British Novelists.* Ed. Harry T. Moore. Carbondale and Edwardsville: Southern Illinois U P, 1967, pp. 59-78.

1556 NOAKES, Aubrey. *Horses, Hounds and Human: Being the Dramatized Story of R. S. Surtees.* London: Oldbourne, 1957.

1557 POPE-HENNESSY, Una. *Durham Company.* London: Chatto & Windus, 1941.

1558 PRITCHETT, V. S. "The Brutal Chivalry." In 87. ("Après moi le garage.")*

1559 STEEL, Anthony. *Jorrocks' England.* New York: Dutton, 1932.

1560 WATSON, Frederick. *Robert Smith Surtees: A Critical Study.* London: Hersant, 1933.

Swinburne, Algernon Charles (1837-1909)

NOVELS

1561 *Love's Cross-Currents. A Year's Letters.* [First pub. by installments in *The Tatler,* Aug. 25-Dec. 29, 1877.] London: Chatto & Windus, 1905. *Lesbia Brandon.* [Printed in incomplete form in 1877; first pub. in 1952. See 1566.]

BIBLIOGRAPHY

1562 EHRSAM, T. G., R. H. DEILY, and R. M. SMITH, eds. In 8, pp. 264-99.

1563 HYDER, Clyde K. "Algernon Charles Swinburne." *The Victorian Poets: A Guide to Research.* Ed. Frederick E. Faverty. Cambridge, Mass.: Harvard U P, 1956, pp. 140-60. (An annotated, selected bibliography.)*

1564 WISE, Thomas J., ed. *A Bibliography of the Writings in Prose and Verse of Algernon Charles Swinburne.* Vol. XX of *Complete Works.* See 1565. (Not entirely reliable.)

COLLECTED AND OTHER EDITIONS OF NOVELS AND LETTERS

1565 *Complete Works.* Eds. Edmund Gosse and Thomas J. Wise. The Bonchurch Edition. 20 vols. New York: Well, 1925-1927.

1566 HUGHES, Randolph. *Lesbia Brandon. An Historical and Critical Commentary, Being Largely a Study (and Elevation) of Swinburne as a Novelist.* London: Falcon, 1952.

1567 LANG, Cecil, ed. *The Swinburne Letters.* 6 vols. New Haven: Yale U P, 1959-1962.*

BIOGRAPHY AND CRITICISM

1568 CHEW, Samuel C. *Swinburne.* Boston: Little, Brown, 1929.

1569 GOSSE, Edmund. *The Life of Algernon Charles Swinburne.* London: Macmillan, 1917.

1570 GRIERSON, H. J. C. *Swinburne*. London: Longmans, Green, 1959.

1571 HARE, Humphrey. *Swinburne: A Biographical Approach*. London: Witherby, 1949.

1572 HYDER, Clyde Kenneth. *Swinburne's Literary Career and Fame*. New York: Russell & Russell, 1963. (With a selected bibliography.)

1573 LAFOURCADE, Georges. *La Jeunesse de Swinburne* (1837-1867). Paris: Société d'édition Les Belles Lettres, 1928.*

1574 LAFOURCADE, Georges. *Swinburne: A Literary Biography*. London: Bell, 1932.

1575 NICOLSON, Harold. *Swinburne*. London: Macmillan, 1926.

1576 NICOLSON, Harold. *Swinburne and Baudelaire*. Oxford: Clarendon P, 1930.

1577 PETERS, Robert L. *The Crowns of Apollo: Swinburne's Principles of Literature and Art*. Detroit: Wayne State U P, 1965.*

1578 WILSON, Edmund, ed. *The Novels of A. C. Swinburne: Love's Cross-Currents and* Lesbia Brandon. New York: Farrar, Straus & Cudahy, 1962. (Contains his essay "Swinburne of Capheaton and Eton," pp. 3-37.)

Taylor, Philip Meadows (1808-1876)

MAIN NOVELS

1579 *The Confessions of a Thug*. 3 vols., 1839. *Tara: A Mahratta Tale*. 3 vols., 1863. *A Noble Queen: A Romance of Indian History*. 3 vols., 1878.

STUDIES

1580 *The Story of My Life*. Ed. by His Daughter. Edinburgh: Blackwood, 1877.

1581 EDWARDES, M. "The Articulate Hero: Philip Meadows Taylor." *Twentieth Century*, 154(1953):209-16.

1582 SINGH, B. "Meadows Taylor and Other Predecessors of Kipling." In 209, pp. 31-67.

Thackeray, Anne Isabella (Lady Ritchie) (1837-1919)

MAIN NOVELS

1583 *The Story of Elizabeth*, 1863. *The Village on the Cliff*, 1867. *Old Kensington*, 1873.

STUDIES

1584 FULLER, H. T., and V. HAMMERSLEY, comps. *Thackeray's Daughter: Some Recollections of Anne Thackeray Ritchie*. Dublin: Euphorion, 1951.

1585 WOOLF, Virginia. "The Enchanted Organ: Anne Thackeray." *The Moment and Other Essays*. London: Hogarth, 1947, pp. 156-68.

Thackeray, William Makepeace (1811-1863)

NOVELS

1586 *The Memoirs of Barry Lyndon: A Romance of the Last Century, by Fitz-Boodle*. [As *The Luck of Barry Lyndon*. 12 nos., *Fraser's Mag*., Jan.-Dec. 1844.] 2 vols. New York: Appleton, 1852. *Vanity Fair: Pen and Pencil Sketches of English Society*. [20 nos., Jan. 1847-July 1848.] As *Vanity Fair, a Novel without a Hero*. London: Bradbury & Evans, 1848. *The History of Pendennis: His Fortunes and Misfortunes, His Friends and Greatest Enemy*. [24 nos., Nov. 1848-Dec. 1850.] 2 vols. London: Bradbury & Evans, 1849-1850. *The History of Henry Esmond, Esq., a Colonel in the Service of Her Majesty Queen Anne*. 3 vols. London: Smith, Elder, 1852. *The Newcomes: Memoirs of a Most Respectable Family*. [24 nos., *Harper's Mag*., Nov. 1853-Oct. 1855.] 2 vols. London: Bradbury & Evans, 1854-1855. *The Virginians. A Tale of the Last Century*. [24 nos., *Harper's Mag*., Dec. 1857-Nov. 1859. 2 vols. London: Bradbury & Evans, 1858-1859.] *Lovel the Widower*. [*Cornhill Mag*., Jan.-June 1860; *Harper's Mag*., Feb.-July 1860.] London: Smith, Elder, 1861. *The Adventures of Philip on His Way through the World*. [20 nos. *Cornhill Mag*., Jan. 1861-Aug. 1862; *Harper's Mag*., Feb. 1861-Sept. 1862.] 3 vols. London: Smith, Elder, 1862. *Denis Duval*. [4 nos. *Cornhill Mag*., March-June 1864; *Harper's Mag*., April, May, July, Aug. 1864.] London: Smith, Elder, 1867.

BIBLIOGRAPHY AND REFERENCE

See 25.*

1587 SHEPHERD, R. H. *The Bibliography of Thackeray: The Published Writings in Prose and Verse and the Sketches and Drawings from 1829-1880*. London: Stock, 1880. Also appended, in a rev. and enl. form, to *Sultan Stork and Other Stories*. Ed. R. H. Shepherd. London: Redway, 1887.)

1588 MUDGE, Isadore Gilbert, and M. Earl SEARS. *A Thackeray Dictionary*. New York: Dutton, 1910.

COLLECTED EDITIONS, LETTERS, ETC.

1589 *Thackeray's Works*. Ed. H. E. Scudder. 22 vols. Boston: Houghton Mifflin, 1889. (Fuller than the English eds.)

1590 *Thackeray's Works*. With biographical introduction by Anne Thackeray Ritchie. 13 vols. New York and London: Harper, 1898-1899. Enl. as Centenary Biographical Edition. 26 vols. 1910-1911.

1591 *Thackeray's Works*. Oxford Edition. 17 vols. Oxford: Oxford U P, 1908. (Introductions by George Saintsbury.)

1592 RAY, Gordon N., ed. *The Letters and Private Papers of William Makepeace Thackeray*. 4 vols. Cambridge, Mass.: Harvard U P, 1945-1946.*

BIOGRAPHICAL AND CRITICAL

1593 CROWE, Eyre. *With Thackeray in America.* New York: Scribner's, 1893.

1594 ELLIS, Geoffrey Uther. *Thackeray.* London: Duckworth, 1933.

1595 GREIG, J. Y. T. *Thackeray: A Reconsideration.* London: Oxford U P, 1950.*

1596 HUNTER, Sir William Wilson. *The Thackerays in India.* London: Frowde, 1897.

1597 LAS VERGNAS, Raymond. *W. M. Thackeray: L'Homme, le penseur, le romancier.* Paris: Champion, 1932.

1598 MELVILLE, Lewis [pseud.]. *William Makepeace Thackeray. A Biography, Including hitherto Uncollected Letters and Speeches and a Bibliography of 1300 Items.* 2 vols. London: Lane, 1910. (Unreliable.)

1599 RAY, Gordon N. *Thackeray.* Vol. I: *The Uses of Adversity, 1811–1846,* (1955); Vol. II: *The Age of Wisdom, 1847–1863* (1958). New York: McGraw-Hill.*

1600 SAINTSBURY, George E. B. *A Consideration of Thackeray.* London: Oxford U P, 1931.*

1601 STEVENSON, Lionel. *The Showman of Vanity Fair.* New York: Scribner's, 1947.

1602 TENNYSON, Sir Charles. "William Makepeace Thackeray, 1811–1863." *EDH,* 33(1965):84–104.

1603 TROLLOPE, A. *Thackeray.* English Men of Letters. New York: Harper, 1879.

1604 WILSON, James Grant. *Thackeray in the United States.* 2 vols. New York: Dodd, Mead, 1904.

CRITICAL

See 75.*

1605 FLAMM, Dudley. *Thackeray's Critics: An Annotated Bibliography of British and American Criticism, 1836–1901.* Chapel Hill: U of North Carolina P, 1967.

1606 TILLOTSON, Geoffrey, and Donald HAWES, eds. *Thackeray: The Critical Heritage.* London: Routledge & Kegan Paul; New York: Barnes & Noble, 1968.

1607 WELSH, Alexander, ed. *Thackeray: A Collection of Critical Essays.* TCV. Englewood Cliffs, N.J.: Prentice-Hall, 1968.

1608 BAGEHOT, Walter. "Sterne and Thackeray." *National Review,* 18(1864):523–53. Repr. *Literary Studies.* London: Longmans, Green, 1879.

1609 BAKER, Joseph E. "Thackeray's Recantation." *PMLA,* 77(1962):586–94.

1610 BETSKY, Seymour. "Society in Thackeray and Trollope." In 39, Vol. VI, pp. 144–68.

1611 COLBY, Robert A. "*Catherine:* Thackeray's Credo." *RES,* 15(1964):381–96.

1612 DODDS, John Wendell. *Thackeray: A Critical Portrait.* New York: Oxford U P, 1941.*

1613 ENNIS, Lambert. *Thackeray, the Sentimental Cynic.* Northwestern U Studies, Humanities Ser. 25. Evanston: Northwestern U P, 1950.

1614 ENZINGER, Philip. "Thackeray, Critic of Literature." *NDQ,* 20(1930):318–33; 21(1931):52–65, 145–61.

1615 GOODELL, Margaret M. *Three Satirists of Snobbery: Thackeray, Meredith, Proust.* Hamburg: Friederichsen, de Gruyter, 1939.

1616 GREIG, J. Y. T. "Thackeray: A Novelist by Accident." In 88, pp. 72–81.*

1617 GULLIVER, Harold S. *Thackeray's Literary Apprenticeship.* Valdosta: Southern Stationery & Printing, 1934.

1618 LESTER, John A., Jr. "Thackeray's Narrative Technique." *PMLA,* 69(1954):392–409.

1619 LOOFBOUROW, John. *Thackeray and the Form of Fiction.* Princeton: Princeton U P, 1964.

1620 MAUSKOPF, Charles. "Thackeray's Attitude toward Dickens' Writings." *NCF,* 21(1966):21–33.

1621 PACEY, W. C. D. "Balzac and Thackeray." *MLR,* 36(1941):213–24.

1622 RADER, Ralph Wilson. "Thackeray's Injustice to Fielding." *JEGP,* 56(1957):203–12.

1623 RAY, Gordon N. *The Buried Life; A Study of the Relations between Thackeray's Fiction and His Personal History.* Cambridge, Mass.: Harvard U P, 1952.*

1624 SENIOR, Nassau. "William Makepeace Thackeray." In 92, pp. 321–96.

1625 SOLOMON, Eric. "Thackeray on War." *VN,* 23(1963):6–11.

1626 STEWART, David H. "Thackeray's Modern Detractors." *Papers of the Michigan Academy of Science, Arts and Letters,* 48(1963):629–38.

1627 SUDRANN, Jean. "The Philosopher's Property: Thackeray and the Use of Time." *VS,* 10(1967):359–88.

1628 TAUBE, Myron. "Thackeray and the Reminiscential Vision." *NCF,* 18(1963):247–59.

1629 TAYLOR, A. Carey. "Balzac et Thackeray." *RLC,* 34(1960):354–69.

1630 TILLOTSON, Geoffrey. *Thackeray the Novelist.* Cambridge: Cambridge U P, 1954.*

1631 TOBIAS, Richard C. "American Criticism of Thackeray, 1848–1855." *NCF,* 8(1953):53–65.

1632 TOUSTER, Eva Beach. "The Literary Relationship of Thackeray and Fielding." *JEGP,* 46(1947):383–94.

1633 VANDIVER, Edward P. "Thackeray and Shakespeare." *Furman Studies,* 34(1951):30–45.

1634 WETHERED, H. N. *On the Art of Thackeray.* London and New York: Longmans, Green, 1938.

Barry Lyndon

1635 *The Memoirs of Barry Lyndon, Esq.* Ed. Robert L. Morris. Lincoln: U of Nebraska P, 1962. (Reprints passages omitted from rev. form.)†

1636 COLBY, Robert A. "*Barry Lyndon* and the Irish Hero." *NCF*, 30(1966):109-30.

Henry Esmond

See 58.

1637 BROGAN, Howard. "Rachel Esmond and the Dilemma of the Victorian Ideal of Womanhood." *ELH*, 13(1946):223-32.

1638 BROWN, John Macmillan. *Esmond, a Study.* Christchurch, N.Z.: Whitcome & Tombs, 1904.

1639 DONNELLY, Jerome. "Stendhal and Thackeray: The Source of *Henry Esmond.*" *RLC*, 39(1965):372-81.

1640 FORSYTHE, Robert S. *A Noble Rake: The Life of Charles, Fourth Lord Mohun.* Cambridge, Mass.: Harvard U P, 1928. (A study of the historical background of *Henry Esmond.*)

1641 HUEY, Grace D. "*Henry Esmond* and the Twentieth Century." *EJ*, 32(1943):456-9.

1642 MARSHALL, William H. "Dramatic Irony in *Henry Esmond.*" *RLV*, 27(1961):35-42.

1643 TILFORD, John E., Jr. "The Love Theme of *Henry Esmond.*" *PMLA*, 67(1952):684-701.

1644 TILFORD, John E., Jr. "The Unsavory Plot of *Henry Esmond.*" *NCF*, 6(1951):121-30.

1645 TILFORD, John E., Jr. "The Untimely Death of Rachel Esmond." *NCF*, 12(1957):148-53.

1646 WILLIAMSON, Karina. "A Note on the Function of Castlewood in *Henry Esmond.*" *NCF*, 18(1963):71-7.

The Newcomes

1647 FRASER, Russell A. "Sentimentality in Thackeray's *The Newcomes.*" *NCF*, 4(1949):187-96.

Pendennis

1648 FIDO, Martin. "*The History of Pendennis:* A Reconsideration." *EIC*, 14(1964):363-79.

1649 IRVINE, William, with Ernest J. SIMMONS and Lyman BRYSON. "William M. Thackeray's *Pendennis.*" *The Invitation to Learning Reader: The Victorian Era.* New York: Random House, 1951.

Vanity Fair

See 48, 52,* 71,* 75,* 97,* 98,* 191.

1650 *Vanity Fair*. Ed. with introduction and notes by Kathleen Tillotson and Geoffrey Tillotson. Boston: Houghton Mifflin, 1963. (First authoritative text.)*†

1651 SUNDELL, M. G., ed. Vanity Fair: *A Collection of Critical Essays*. TCI. Englewood Cliffs, N.J.: Prentice-Hall, 1969.†

1652 RANDALL, David A. "Notes Toward a Correct Collation of the First Edition of *Vanity Fair*." *PBSA*, 42(1948):95-109.

1653 BAKER, Joseph E. "*Vanity Fair* and the Celestial City." *NCF*, 10(1955):89-98.

1654 BLODGETT, Harriet. "Necessary Presence: The Rhetoric of the Narrator in *Vanity Fair*." *NCF*, 22(1967):211-23.

1655 BORT, Barry D. "Dove or Serpent?—The Imposter in *Vanity Fair*." *Discourse*, 9(1966):482-91.

1656 CHESTERTON, Gilbert Keith. *A Handful of Authors*. New York: Sheed & Ward, 1953, pp. 56-65.*

1657 CRAIG, G. Armour. "On the Style of *Vanity Fair*." *Style in Prose Fiction*. English Institute Essays. Ed. Harold C. Martin. New York: Columbia U P, 1959, pp. 87-113.*

1658 DYSON, A. E. "*Vanity Fair:* An Irony against Heroes." *CritQ*, 6(1964):11-31. Repr. in 450.

1659 FRASER, Russell A. "Pernicious Casuistry: A Study of Character in *Vanity Fair*." *NCF*, 12(1957):137-47.

1660 GREENE, D. J. "Becky Sharp and Lord Steyne—Thackeray or Disraeli." *NCF*, 16(1961):157-64.

1661 HANNAH, Donald. " 'The Author's Own Candles': The Significance of the Illustrations to *Vanity Fair*." *Renaissance and Modern Essays Presented to Vivian de Sola Pinto*. Ed. G. R. Hibbard. London: Routledge & Kegan Paul, 1966, pp. 129-36.

1662 JOHNSON, E. D. H. "*Vanity Fair* and *Amelia:* Thackeray in the Perspective of the Eighteenth Century." *MP*, 59(1961):100-13.

1663 MATHISON, John K. "The German Sections of *Vanity Fair*." *NCF*, 18(1963):235-46.

1664 PARIS, Bernard J. "The Psychic Structure of *Vanity Fair*." *VS*, 10(1967):389-410.*

1665 RAY, Gordon N. "*Vanity Fair:* One Version of the Novelist's Responsibility." *EDH*, n.s.25(1950):87-101.

1666 SHARP, Sister M. Corona, O. S. U. "Sympathetic Mockery: A Study of the Narrator's Character in *Vanity Fair*." *ELH*, 29(1962):324-36.

1667 SHERBO, Arthur. "A Suggestion for the Original of Thackeray's Rawdon Crawley." *NCF*, 10(1955):211-16.

1668 SPILKA, Mark. "A Note on Thackeray's Amelia." *NCF*, 10(1955):202-10.

1669 STEVENS, Joan. "Thackeray's *Vanity Fair*." *REL*, 6(1965):19-38.

1670 STEVENSON, Lionel. "*Vanity Fair* and Lady Morgan." *PMLA*, 48(1933):547-51.

1671 STEWART, David H. "*Vanity Fair:* Life in the Void." *CE*, 25(1963):209-14.

1672 TALON, Henri A. "Thackeray's *Vanity Fair* Revisited: Fiction as Truth." *Of Books and Humankind.* Ed. John Butt. London: Routledge & Kegan Paul, 1964, pp. 117-48.

1673 TAUBE, Myron. "The Character of Amelia and the Meaning of *Vanity Fair.*" *VN*, 18(1960):1-8.

1674 TAUBE, Myron. "Contrast as a Principle of Structure in *Vanity Fair.*" *NCF*, 18(1963):119-35.

1675 TAUBE, Myron. "The George-Amelia-Dobbin Triangle in the Structure of *Vanity Fair.*" *VN*, 29(1966):9-18.

1676 TAUBE, Myron. "The Race for Money in the Structure of *Vanity Fair.*" *VN*, 24(1963):12-17.

1677 TAUBE, Myron. "Thackeray at Work: The Significance of Two Deletions from *Vanity Fair.*" *NCF*, 18(1963):273-9.

1678 TILFORD, John E., Jr. "The Degradation of Becky Sharp." *SAQ*, 58(1959):603-08.

1679 VON HENDY, Andrew. "Misunderstandings about Becky's Characterization in *Vanity Fair.*" *NCF*, 18(1963):279-83.

1680 WAGENKNECHT, Edward. "The Selfish Heroine: Thackeray and Galsworthy." *CE*, 4(1943):293-8.

1681 WILKINSON, Ann Y. "The Tomeavesian Way of Knowing the World: Technique and Meaning in *Vanity Fair.*" *ELH*, 32(1965):370-87.

THE VIRGINIANS

1682 GRAHAM, W. H. "Thackeray's *The Virginians.*" *FR*, 167(1945):45-8.

1683 HUBBELL, Jay B. "Thackeray and Virginia." *VQR*, 3(1927):78-86.

Trollope, Anthony (1815-1882)

NOVELS

1684 *The Macdermots of Ballycloran.* 3 vols. London: Newby, 1847. *The Kellys and the O'Kellys: A Tale of Irish Life.* 3 vols. London: Colburn, 1848. *La Vendée: An Historical Romance.* 3 vols. London: Colburn, 1850. *The Warden.* London: Longman, Brown, Green & Longmans, 1855. *Barchester Towers.* 3 vols. London: Longman, Brown, Green, Longmans & Roberts, 1857. *The Three Clerks.* 3 vols. London: Bentley, 1858. *Doctor Thorne.* 3 vols. London: Chapman & Hall, 1858. *The Bertrams.* 3 vols. London: Chapman & Hall, 1859. *Castle Richmond.* 3 vols. London: Chapman & Hall, 1860. *Framley Parsonage.* 3 vols. [*Cornhill Mag.*, Jan. 1860-April 1861.] London: Smith, Elder, 1861. *Orley Farm.* [20 nos., March 1861-Oct. 1862.] 2 vols. London: Chapman & Hall, 1862. *Rachel Ray.* 2 vols. London: Chapman & Hall, 1863. *The Small House at Allington.* [*Cornhill Mag.*, Sept. 1862-April 1864.] 2 vols. London: Smith, Elder, 1864. *Can You Forgive Her?* [20 nos., Jan. 1864-Aug. 1865.] 2 vols. London: Chapman & Hall, 1864. *Miss Mackenzie.* 2 vols. London: Chapman & Hall, 1865. *The Belton Estate.* [*Fortnightly Rev.*, May 1865-Jan. 1866.] London: Chapman & Hall, 1866.

1685 *Nina Balatka: The Story of a Maiden of Prague.* [*Blackwood's,* July 1866–Jan. 1867.] 2 vols. Edinburgh and London: Blackwood, 1867. *The Last Chronicle of Barset.* [32 nos., Dec. 1866–July 1867.] 2 vols. London: Smith, Elder, 1867. *The Claverings.* [*Cornhill Mag.,* Feb. 1866–May 1867.] 2 vols. London: Smith, Elder, 1867. *Linda Tressel.* [*Blackwood's,* 1867–1868.] 2 vols. Edinburgh and London: Blackwood, 1868. *Phineas Finn, the Irish Member.* [*St. Paul's Mag.,* Oct. 1867–May 1869.] 2 vols. London: Virtue, 1869. *He Knew He Was Right.* [32 nos., Oct. 1868–May 1869.] 2 vols. London: Stone, Strahan, 1869. *The Vicar of Bullhampton.* [11 nos., July 1869–May 1870.] 2 vols. London: Bradbury, Evans, 1870. *Sir Harry Hotspur of Humblethwaite.* [*Macmillan's Mag.,* May 1870–Dec. 1870.] London: Hurst & Blackett, 1871. *Ralph the Heir.* [19 nos., Jan. 1870–July 1871.] 3 vols. London: Hurst & Blackett, 1871. *The Golden Lion of Granpere.* [*Good Words,* Jan. 1872–Aug. 1872.] London: Tinsley, 1872. *The Eustace Diamonds.* [*Fortnightly Rev.,* July 1871–Feb. 1873.] 3 vols. London: Chapman & Hall, 1873. *Phineas Redux.* [*Graphic,* July 1873–Jan. 1874.] 2 vols. London: Chapman & Hall, 1874. *Lady Anna.* [*Fortnightly Rev.,* April 1873–April 1874.] 2 vols. London: Chapman & Hall, 1874. *Harry Heathcote of Gangoil: A Tale of Australian Bush Life.* [*Graphic,* Christmas Number, Dec. 25, 1873.] London: Low, 1874. *The Way We Live Now.* [20 nos., Feb. 1874–Sept. 1875.] 2 vols. London: Chapman & Hall, 1875. *The Struggle of Brown, Jones, and Robinson by One of the Firm.* [First pub. in *Cornhill Mag.,* Aug. 1861–March 1862.] London: Smith, Elder, 1870. *The Prime Minister.* [8 nos., Nov. 1875–June 1876.] 4 vols. London: Chapman & Hall, 1876. *The American Senator.* [*Temple Bar Mag.,* May 1876–July 1877.] 3 vols. London: Chapman & Hall, 1877. *The Lady of Launay.* New York: Harper, 1878. *Is He Popenjoy?* [*All the Year Round,* Oct. 1877–July 1878.] 3 vols. London: Chapman & Hall, 1878. *An Eye for an Eye.* [*Whitehall Rev.,* Aug. 1878–Feb. 1879.] 2 vols. London: Chapman & Hall, 1879. *Cousin Henry.* [*Manchester Weekly Times Supp.,* March 1879–May 1879.] 2 vols. London: Chapman & Hall, 1879. *John Caldigate.* [*Blackwood's,* April 1878–June 1879.] 3 vols. London: Chapman & Hall, 1879. *The Duke's Children.* [*All the Year Round,* Oct. 1879–July 1880.] 3 vols. London: Chapman & Hall, 1880. *Dr. Wortle's School.* [*Blackwood's,* May 1880–Dec. 1880.] 2 vols. London: Chapman & Hall, 1881. *Ayala's Angel.* 2 vols. London: Chapman & Hall, 1881. *The Fixed Period.* [*Blackwood's,* Oct. 1881–March 1882.] 2 vols. Edinburgh and London: Blackwood, 1882. *Marian Fay.* [*Graphic,* Dec. 1881–June 1882.] 3 vols. London: Chapman & Hall, 1882. *Kept in the Dark.* [*Good Words,* May 1882–Dec. 1882.] 2 vols. London: Chatto & Windus, 1882. *Mr. Scarborough's Family.* [*All the Year Round,* May–June 1883.] 3 vols. London: Chatto & Windus, 1883. *The Landleaguers.* [*Life,* Nov. 1882–Oct. 1883.] 3 vols. London: Chatto & Windus, 1883. *An Old Man's Love.* 2 vols. Edinburgh and London: Blackwood, 1884.

BIBLIOGRAPHY AND REFERENCE

See 25.*

1686 CHAPMAN, R. W. "The Text of Trollope's Novels." *RES,* 17(1941):322–31.

1687 SADLEIR, Michael. *Trollope: A Bibliography.* London: Constable, 1928. [Rev. 1934; repr. 1964.]*

1688 BOOTH, Bradford A. "Anthony Trollope." *VN,* 13(1958):24–5. (Guide to research materials.)

1689 GEROULD, Winifred G., and James T. GEROULD. *A Guide to Trollope.* Princeton: Princeton U P, 1948.

1690 HELLING, Rafael. *A Century of Trollope Criticism.* Helsingfors: Kennikat, 1956. (Useful bibliography of criticism.)

COLLECTIONS, LETTERS, ETC.

There is no complete edition: Dodd Mead published a useful collection under the titles "The Barsetshire Novels," "The Manor House Novels," and "The Parliamentary Novels." The best collection is probably the Oxford Illustrated Edition. WC has the largest number of Trollope's novels in print. There are many paperback reprints, especially of the Barchester Novels; those with useful apparatus are listed below under their titles.

1691 *The Barsetshire Novels of Anthony Trollope.* Ed. Michael Sadleir. 14 vols. Stratford-upon-Avon: Shakespeare Head, 1929.

1692 *The Oxford Illustrated Trollope.* Crown Edition. Ed. Michael Sadleir and F. Page. 15 vols. London: Oxford U P, 1948. (Not completed.)

1693 Trollope, Anthony. *An Autobiography.* Ed. F. Page. London and New York: Oxford U P, 1950.*

1694 *The Letters of Anthony Trollope.* Ed. Bradford A. Booth. London and New York: Oxford U P, 1951.*

BIOGRAPHICAL AND GENERAL

1695 BOOTH, Bradford A. *Anthony Trollope: Aspects of His Life and Art.* Bloomington: Indiana U P, 1958.*

1696 BROWN, Beatrice Curtis. *Anthony Trollope.* London: Barker, 1950.

1697 DAVIES, Hugh Sykes. *Trollope.* WTW. New York and London: Longmans, Green, 1960.†

1698 ESCOTT, T. H. S. *Anthony Trollope: His Work, Associates, and Literary Originals.* London and New York: Lane, 1913.

1699 STEBBINS, Lucy Poate, and Richard P. STEBBINS. *The Trollopes: The Chronicle of a Writing Family.* New York: Columbia U P, 1945.*

1700 TINGAY, Lance O. "Trollope and the Beverly Election." *NCF,* 5(1950):23–38.

CRITICAL

See 39,* 52,* 105, 201,* 205.

1701 SMALLEY, Donald A., ed. *Trollope: The Critical Heritage.* New York: Barnes & Noble, 1969.

1702 AITKEN, David. "'A Kind of Felicity': Some Notes about Trollope's Style." *NCF,* 20(1966):337–53.

1703 BANKS, J. A. "*The Way They Lived Then:* Anthony Trollope and the 1870's." *VS,* 12(1968):177–200.

1704 BOLL, Ernest. "The Infusion of Dickens in Trollope." *Trollopian* (see 18), 3(1946):11–24.

1705 BOOTH, Bradford A. "Trollope on the Novel." *Essays Critical and Historical Dedicated to Lily B. Campbell.* Berkeley: U of California P, 1950.

1706 BORINSKY, Ludwig. "Trollope's Barsetshire Novels." *NS*, (1962):533-53.

1707 BORINSKY, Ludwig. "Trollope's Palliser Novels." *NS*, (1963):389-407.

1708 BOWEN, Elizabeth. *Anthony Trollope: A New Judgment.* New York and London: Oxford U P, 1946.

1709 BRACE, Gerald Warner. "The World of Anthony Trollope." *TQ*, 4(1961):180-9.

1710 BRADFORD, Gamaliel. *A Naturalist of Souls.* New York: Dodd, Mead, 1917; Boston and New York: Houghton Mifflin, 1926.

1711 BURN, W. L. "Anthony Trollope's Politics." *Nineteenth Century*, 143(1948):161-71.

1712 BURN, W. L. "Surtees and Trollope." *Blackwood's*, 261(1947):301-7.

1713 CADBURY, William. "Shape and Theme: Determinants of Trollope's Forms." *PMLA*, 78(1963):326-32.

1714 CHAMBERLAIN, David S. "Unity and Irony in Trollope's *Can You Forgive Her?*" *SEL*, 8(1968):669-80.

1715 CHAPMAN, R. W. "Personal Names in Trollope's Political Novels." In 161, pp. 72-81.

1716 COCKSHUT, A. O. J. *Anthony Trollope: A Critical Study.* Fair Lawn, N.J.: Essential Books, 1956.*†

1717 COYLE, William. "Trollope and the Bi-Columned Shakespeare." *NCF*, 6(1951):33-46. (Study of Trollope's use of literary allusions.)

1718 COYLE, William. "Trollope as Social Anthropologist." *CE*, 17(1956):392-7.

1719 DAVIES, Hugh Sykes. "Trollope and His Style." *REL*, I(1960):73-85.

1720 DUSTIN, John E. "Thematic Alternation in Trollope." *PMLA*, 77(1962):280-8.

1721 FRASER, Russell A. "Anthony Trollope's Younger Characters." *NCF*, 6(1951):96-106.

1722 GRAGG, Wilson B. "Trollope and Carlyle." *NCF*, 13(1958):266-70.

1723 HAGAN, John. "The Divided Mind of Anthony Trollope." *NCF*, 14(1959):1-26.

1724 HOLLIS, Christopher. "The Meaning of Anthony Trollope." *For Hilaire Belloc.* Ed. Douglas Woodruff. London: Sheed & Ward, 1942.

1725 JAMES, Henry. "Anthony Trollope." *Century*, 28(1883):384-95. (Later collected in *Partial Portraits* [1888], and *The Future of the Novel* [1956].)*†

1726 KER, W. P. "Anthony Trollope" [1906]. *On Modern Literature: Lectures and Addresses.* Eds. Terence Spencer and James Sutherland. Oxford: Clarendon P, 1955.

1727 KNOX, R. A. "A Ramble in Barsetshire." *LMerc* 5(1922):378-85.

1728 KOETS, C. C. *Female Characters in the Works of Anthony Trollope.* Gouda: van Tilburg, 1933.

1729 LASKI, Audrey L. "Myths of Character: An Aspect of the Novel." *NCF,* 14(1960):333-44.

1730 MIZENER, Arthur. "Anthony Trollope: The Palliser Novels." See 88, pp. 160-76.*

1731 MORE, Paul Elmer. *The Demon of the Absolute.* Princeton: Princeton U P, 1929. (Includes, oddly enough, a chapter on Trollope.)

1732 MORGAN, Charles. *The Liberties of the Mind.* New York: Macmillan, 1951.

1733 O'CONNOR, Frank [pseud.]. "Trollope the Realist." *The Mirror in the Roadway.* New York: Knopf, 1956, pp. 165-83.*

1734 PARKS, Edd W. "Trollope and the Defence of Exegesis." *NCF,* 7(1953):265-71.

1735 POLHEMUS, Robert M. *The Changing World of Anthony Trollope.* Berkeley and Los Angeles: U of California P, 1968.*

1736 ROBBINS, F. E. "Chronology and History in Trollope's Barset and Parliamentary Novels." *NCF,* 5(1951):303-16.

1737 ROBINSON, Clement F. "Trollope's Jury Trials." *NCF,* 6(1952):247-68.

1738 ROUTH, H. V. *Towards the Twentieth Century: Essays in the Spiritual History of the Nineteenth Century* [1937]. New York: Macmillan, 1938.

1739 SADLEIR, Michael. *Trollope: A Commentary* [1927]. Rev. ed. London: Constable, 1945.*†

1740 SAINTSBURY, George. *Corrected Impressions.* London: Heinemann, 1895. (Includes an essay on Trollope.)

1741 SAINTSBURY, George. "Trollope Revisited." *E&S,* 6(1920):41-66.

1742 SHERMAN, T. A. "The Financial Motive in the Barchester Novels." *CE,* 9(1948):413-18.

1743 SKINNER, E. L. "Mr. Trollope's Young Ladies." *NCF,* 4(1949):197-207.

1744 SLAKEY, Roger L. "Melmotte's Death: A Prism of Meaning in *The Way We Live Now.*" *ELH,* 34(1967):248-59.

1745 SMITH, Sheila M. "Anthony Trollope: The Novelist as Moralist." *Renaissance and Modern Essays Presented to Vivian de Sola Pinto.* Ed. G. R. Hibbard. London: Routledge & Kegan Paul, 1966, pp. 129-36.

1746 TANNER, Tony. "Trollope's *The Way We Live Now:* Its Modern Significance." *CritQ,* 9(1967):256-71.

1747 THALE, Jerome. "The Problem of Structure in Trollope." *NCF,* 15(1960):147-57.

1748 TILLOTSON, Geoffrey. "Trollope's Style." *BSTCF,* 2(1961):3-6.

1749 TINKER, Chauncey Brewster. "Trollope." *YR,* 36(1947):424-34. Repr. in *Essays in Retrospect.* New Haven: Yale U P, 1948.

1750 WALPOLE, Hugh. *Anthony Trollope.* London: Macmillan, 1928.

1751 WELLSBY, Paul A. "Anthony Trollope and the Church of England." *CQR*, 163(1962):210-20.

1752 WILDMAN, John Hazard. *Anthony Trollope's England*. Providence: Brown U P, 1940.

1753 WILDMAN, John Hazard. "Anthony Trollope Today." *CE*, 7(1946):397-9.

1754 SADLEIR, Michael. *Things Past*. London: Constable, 1944. (Includes collection of introductions to Shakespeare Head Edition of Trollope's novels.)*

AMERICAN SENATOR

1755 HARDEN, Edgar F. "The Alien Voice: Trollope's Western Senator." *TSLL*, 8(1966):219-34.

1756 STRYKER, David. "The Significance of Trollope's *American Senator*." *NCF*, 5(1950):141-9.

1757 WILDMAN, John Hazard. "Trollope Illustrates the Distinction." *NCF*, 4(1949):101-10.

BARCHESTER TOWERS

See 1773.

1758 *Barchester Towers*. Ed. Bradford A. Booth. New York: Holt, Rinehart, 1949.†

1759 CADBURY, William. "Character and the Mock Heroic in *Barchester Towers*." *TSLL*, 5(1964):509-19.

1760 SHAW, W. David. "Moral Drama in *Barchester Towers*." *NCF*, 19(1964):45-54.

CAN YOU FORGIVE HER?

1761 HOYT, Norris D. "*Can You Forgive Her*: A Commentary." *Trollopian* (see 18), 2(1947):57-70.

COUSIN HENRY

1762 POLHEMUS, Robert M. "*Cousin Henry*: Trollope's Note from Underground." *NCF*, 20(1966):385-9.

DR. THORNE

1763 *Dr. Thorne*. Ed. with introd. Elizabeth Bowen. Boston: Houghton Mifflin, 1960.†

1764 DIXON, Sir Owen. "Sir Roger Scatcherd's Will, in Anthony Trollope's *Doctor Thorne*." *Jesting Pilate and Other Papers and Addresses*. Sydney: Law Book, 1965, pp. 71-81.

1765 SADLEIR, Michael. "A Trollope Love-Story; Mary Thorne." *Nineteenth Century*, 96(1924):355-66.

THE DUKE'S CHILDREN

1766 HAGAN, John. "*The Duke's Children*: Trollope's Psychological Masterpiece." *NCF*, 13(1958):1-21.

THE EUSTACE DIAMONDS

1767 MILLEY, H. J. W. "*The Eustace Diamonds* and *The Moonstone.*" *SP*, 36(1939):651-63.

THE KELLYS AND THE O'KELLYS

1768 DONOVAN, Robert A. "Trollope's 'Prentice Work.' " *MP*, 53(1956):179-86.

THE LAST CHRONICLE OF BARSET

See also 1771.

1769 *The Last Chronicle of Barset.* Ed. Arthur Mizener. Boston: Houghton Mifflin, 1966.†

ORLEY FARM

1770 ADAMS, Robert M. "*Orley Farm* and Real Fiction." *NCF*, 8(1953):27-41.

1771 BOOTH, Bradford A. "Trollope's *Orley Farm:* Artistry Manqué." In 88, pp. 146-59. (Compares *Orley Farm* with *The Last Chronicle of Barset.*)

PHINEAS FINN

1772 BLOOMFIELD, Morton W. "Trollope's Use of Canadian History in *Phineas Finn.*" *NCF*, 5(1950):67-74.

THE WARDEN

1773 *The Warden and Barchester Towers.* Ed. Louis Auchincloss. Boston: Houghton Mifflin, 1966.†

1774 ARNOLD, Ralph. *The Whiston Matter.* London: Hart-Davis, 1961.

1775 BEST, G. F. A. "The Road to Hiram's Hospital." *VS*, 5(1961):135-50.

1776 GOLDBERG, M. A. "Trollope's *The Warden:* A Commentary on the 'Age of Equipoise.' " *NCF*, 17(1963):381-90.

1777 HAWKINS, Sherman. "Mr. Harding's Church Music." *ELH*, 29(1962):202-23.

1778 STEVENSON, Lionel. "Dickens and the Origin of *The Warden.*" *NCF*, 2(1947):83-9.

Trollope, Frances, née Milton (1780-1863)

MAIN NOVELS

1779 *The Refugee in America.* 3 vols., 1832. *The Life and Adventures of Jonathan Jefferson Whitlaw; or, Scenes on the Mississippi.* 3 vols., 1836. *The Vicar of Wrexhill.* 3 vols., 1837. *The Widow Barnaby.* 3 vols., 1839. *The Life and Adventures of Michael Armstrong, the Factory Boy.* 3 vols., 1840. *The Barnabys in America; or, Adventures of the Widow Wedded.* 3 vols., 1843. *Jessie Phillips: A Tale of the Present Day.* 3 vols., 1843. *Petticoat Government.* 3 vols., 1850.

STUDIES

1780 BIGLAND, Eileen. *The Indomitable Mrs. Trollope.* London: Barry, 1953.

1781 TROLLOPE, F. E. *Frances Trollope: Her Life and Literary Work.* 2 vols. London: Bentley, 1895.

Ward, Mrs. Humphry (Mary Augusta, née Arnold) (1851–1920)

MAIN NOVELS

1782 *Miss Bretherton,* 1881. *Robert Elsmere.* 3 vols., 1888. *The History of David Grieve.* 3 vols., 1892. *The Marriage of William Ashe,* 1905. *The Case of Richard Meynell,* 1911.

STUDIES

See 61.

1783 *The Writings of Mrs. Humphry Ward.* With introductions by the author. 16 vols. Boston: Houghton Mifflin, 1911–1912. (Incomplete.)

1784 WARD, Mrs. Humphry. *A Writer's Recollections.* New York: Harper, 1918.

1785 TREVELYAN, Janet Penrose. *Life of Mrs. Humphry Ward.* London: Constable, 1923. (By her daughter.)

1786 KNOEPFLMACHER, U. C. "The Rival Ladies: Mrs. Ward's *Lady Connie* and Lawrence's *Lady Chatterley's Lover.*" *VS,* 4(1960):141–58.

1787 LEDERER, C. "Mary Arnold Ward and the Victorian Ideal." *NCF,* 6(1951):201–08.

1788 RYALS, Clyde de L. Introduction to *Robert Elsmere.* Lincoln: Nebraska U P, 1967.†

1789 WILLEY, Basil. "How *Robert Elsmere* Struck Some Contemporaries." *E&S,* n.s. 10(1957):53–68.

Watts-Dunton, Theodore (1832–1914)

MAIN NOVELS

1790 *Aylwin,* 1899. *Vesprie Towers,* 1916.

STUDIES

1791 BENSON, A. C. "Theodore Watts-Dunton." *Life and Letters* (1932). Repr. in *English Critical Essays: Twentieth Century.* WC. London: Oxford U P, 1933, pp. 129–145.

1792 TRUSS, Tom J. "Theodore Watts-Dunton: A Primary Bibliography." *BB,* 27(1961):114–17.

Whyte-Melville, George John (1821–1878)

MAIN NOVELS

1793 *Captain Digby Grand. An Autobiography.* 2 vols., 1853. *Kate Coventry: An Autobiography,* 1856. *Market Harborough; or, How Mr. Sawyer Went to the Shires,* 1861. *The Gladiators: A Tale of Rome and Judea,* 1863. *Katerfelto. A Story of Exmoor,* 1875.

STUDY

1794 FORTESCUE, Sir John. "George Whyte-Melville." In 37.

Wood, Mrs. Henry, née Ellen Price (1814–1887)

MAIN NOVELS

1795 *Danesbury House,* 1860. *East Lynne.* 3 vols., 1861. *Mrs. Halliburton's Troubles.* 3 vols., 1862. *The Channings.* 3 vols., 1862. *Roland Yorke.* 3 vols. 1869.

STUDIES

See 62.

1796 WOOD, Charles W. *Memorials of Mrs. Henry Wood.* London: Bentley, 1894.

Yonge, Charlotte Mary (1823–1901)

MAIN NOVELS

1797 *The Heir of Redclyffe.* 2 vols. 1853. *Heartsease: or, The Brother's Wife,* 1854. *The Lances of Lynwood,* 1855. *The Daisy Chain; or, Aspirations. A Family Chronicle.* 2 vols., 1856. *Dynevor Terrace.* 2 vols., 1857. *The Trial: More Links of the Daisy Chain.* 2 vols., 1864. *The Clever Woman of the Family.* 2 vols., 1865. *The Dove in the Eagle's Nest.* 2 vols., 1866. *Unknown to History,* 1882.

STUDIES

1798 BATTISCOMBE, Georgina. *Charlotte Mary Yonge: The Story of an Uneventful Life.* London: Constable, 1943.

1799 COLERIDGE, Christabel. *Charlotte Mary Yonge: Her Life and Letters.* London: Macmillan, 1903.

1800 LASKI, Marghanita, and Georgina BATTISCOMBE. *A Chaplet for Charlotte Yonge.* Chester Springs, Pa.: Dufour Editions, 1965. (Collection of critical essays.)

1801 LEAVIS, Q. D. "Charlotte Yonge and Christian Discrimination." *Scrutiny*, 12(1944):152-60.

1802 MARE, Margaret, and A. O. PERCIVAL. *Victorian Best-Seller: The World of Charlotte Yonge.* London: Harrap, 1948.

MINOR AND OCCASIONAL NOVELISTS (ARRANGED ALPHABETICALLY)

1803 Ballantyne, Robert Michael (1825-1894). Barrowcliffe, A. J. (Albert Julius Mott), (fl. 1856-1873). Bede, Cuthbert (Edward Bradley), (1827-1889). Black, William (1841-1898). Bray, Anna Eliza, née Kempe (1790-1883). Brooks, Charles William Shirley (1816-1874). Brown, Oliver Madox (1855-1874). Buchanan, Robert (1841-1901). Bulwer-Lytton, Lady Rosina, née Wheeler (1804-1882). Burnett, Frances Hodgson (1849-1924). Bury, Lady Charlotte Susan Maria, née Campbell (1775-1861). Cavanagh, Julia (1824-1877). Chamier, Frederick (1796-1870). Chorley, Henry Fothergill (1808-1872). Clive, Caroline, née Meysey-Wigley (1801-1873). Cockton, Henry (1807-1853). Collins, Charles Alston (1828-1873). Collins, Mortimer (1827-1876). Conway, Hugh (Frederick John Fargus), (1847-1885). Cooper, Thomas (1805-1892). Croly, George (1780-1860). Crowe, Catherine, née Stevens (1800-1876). Cunningham, Allan (1784-1842). Dallas, Robert Charles (1754-1824). Ellis, Sarah, née Stickney (ca. 1810-1872). Ewing, Juliana Horatia, née Gatty (1841-1885). Falconer, Lanoe (Mary Hawker), (1848-1908). Fane, Violet (Mary Montgomerie Lamb, later Singleton, later Lady Currie), (1843-1905). Farjeon, Benjamin Leopold (1838-1905). Fitzgerald, Percy Hetherington (1834-1925). Fraser, James Baillie (1783-1856). Froude, James Anthony (1818-1894). Fullerton, Lady Georgina Charlotte (1812-1885). Gaspey, Thomas (1788-1871). Gatty, Margaret (1807-1873). Grant, James (1822-1887). Grattan, Thomas Colley (1792-1864). Hall, Anna Maria, née Fielding (1800-1881). Hamilton, Elizabeth (1758-1816). Hamilton, Thomas (1789-1842). Hatton, Joseph (1841-1907). Helps, Sir Arthur (1813-1875). Henty, George Alfred (1832-1902). Hockley, William Browne (1792-1860). Hook, James (1771-1828). Hoole, Barbara, (afterwards Hofland), née Wreaks (1770-1844). Hope, Thomas (1770-1831). Howard, Edward George Granville (?-1841). Howitt, Mary, née Botham (1799-1888). Howitt, William (1792-1879). Johnstone, Christian Isobel (1781-1857). Lamb, Lady Caroline, née Ponsonby (1785-1828). Lang, Andrew (1844-1912). Lathom, Francis (1777-1832). Lawless, Emily (1845-1913). Lee, Holme (Harriet Parr), (1828-1900). Lewes, George Henry (1817-1878). Lister, Thomas Henry (1800-1842). Lockhart, John Gibson (1794-1854). Manning, Anne (1807-1879). Marsh, Anne, later Marsh-Caldwell, née Caldwell (1791-1874). Maxwell, William Hamilton (1792-1850). Mayhew, Augustus Septimus (1826-1875). Minto, William (1845-1893). Moir, David Macbeth (1798-1851). Molesworth, Mary Louisa, née Stewart (early works under pseud. Ennis Graham), (1839-1921). Mudford, William (1782-1848). Murray, Sir Charles Augustus (1806-1895). Neale, William Johnson (1812-1893). Newman, John Henry, Cardinal (1801-1890). Noel, Lady Augusta (1838-1902). Norton, Caroline (1808-1877). Oliphant, Laurence (1829-1888). Payn, James (1830-1898). Phillips, Samuel (1814-1854). Phipps, Constantine Henry, Marquis of Normanby (1797-1863). Picken, Andrew (1788-1833). Porter, Anna Maria (1780-1832).

1804 Porter, Jane (1776-1850). Reynolds, George William McArthur (1814-1879). Rice, James (1843-1882). Riddell, Mrs. J. H. (Charlotte Elizabeth Lawson Cowan), (1832-1906). Ruffini, John (Giovanni Domenico Ruffini), (1807-1881). Russell, William Clark (1844-1911). St. Leger, Francis Barry Boyle (1799-1829). Scargill, William Pitt (1787-1836). Scott, Michael (1789-1835). Sewell, Anna (1820-1878). Sewell, Elizabeth Missing (1815-1906). Shee, Sir Martin Archer (1769-1850). Simpson, John Palgrave (1807-1887). Sinclair, Catherine (1800-1864). Smart, Henry Hawley (1833-1893). Smedley, Francis Edward (1818-1864). Smith, Albert (1816-1860). Smith, Horatio (1779-1849). Sterling, John (1806-1844). Tautphoeus, Baroness Jemima, née Montgomery (1807-1893). Trollope, Thomas Adolphus (1810-1892). Tytler, Christina Catherine (b. 1848). Veley, Margaret (1843-1887). Warburton, Eliot (1810-1852). Ward, Robert, afterwards Plumer Ward (1765-1846). Warren, Samuel (1807-1877). Waugh, Edwin (1817-1890). Wills, William Gorman (1828-1891). Yates, Edmund Hodgson (1831-1894).

NOTES

INDEX

INDEX

INDEX

INDEX

INDEX

INDEX

INDEX

INDEX

INDEX

INDEX